Copyright © 2020

Calmmother Limited, Tereza Fonda, Dr. Pamela Smith, ND

All rights reserved.

No part of this book may be reproduced, or stored in a retrieval system, or transmitted in any form or by any means, electronic, mechanical, photocopying, recording, or otherwise, without express written permission of the co-authors and publisher.

Important notice to reader: This book, and all other information and resources available at www.calmmother.com, are designed for general informational and educational purposes only. They are not intended to provide, and do not constitute, medical, health, legal, investment, financial or other professional advice. Always consult your qualified healthcare provider (healthcare provider) about your and your baby's health and wellness. For more information, view the Terms & Conditions at www.calmmother.com.

Calmmother
Modern Method for Mothers

Rob yourself of sleep and you'll find you do not function at your personal best.

Arianna Huffington

Table of contents

Introduction	4
About this program	5
Offering parents a solution to sleep deprivation	7
Creating a consistent schedule to avoid sleep training later	8
Baby care basics	10
Balancing baby and self care	11
Your baby's sleep cycle	12
Communicating with your baby	15
Healthy feeding and sleep practices and more	17
Quick reference guide for baby feeding and sleep	17
Healthy feeding practices	19
Healthy sleep practices	44
Baby feeding and sleep schedule	57
Phase 1: Weeks 1 and 2 – surviving the first two weeks	59
Phase 2: Weeks 3 to 7 – establishing your schedule	64
Phase 3: Weeks 8 to 11 – maintain routine & drop feedings	66
Phase 4: Week 12 (three months) on – sleep through the night	69
Six to 12 months: Solids – maintain sleeping through the night	73
Other important things	75
Feeding and sleep one year onward	75
Baby essentials and safety	77
Potty training	90
Discipline and conscious parenting	91
Finding the right childcare for your family (newborn on)	93
Closing	94
Notes & supplemental documents	95
Blank chart for your baby	96
Sample baby charts for each phase	97
FAQs about the baby feeding and sleep program	102
Acknowledgments	110

Introduction

Having a baby is a big deal even if you already have kids! Each child is different and there is no one right way to navigate through parenthood.

This baby feeding and sleep program summarizes the important information and tips to guide parents through the first year after birth. Our tested feeding and sleep schedule helps make days and nights more predictable and manageable as you gently transition your baby to a flexible schedule that works for your family (and an uninterrupted night of sleep between 10 to 12 weeks). Establish your healthy feeding and sleep practices after childbirth, or when it works for your family!

Visit Calmmother.com for must know information and tips to help you make informed decisions about your health and your family's health.

About this program

This program is helpful to first time and experienced parents as well as other caregivers because it outlines important information and tips for life with a new baby. Our baby feeding and sleep program is a tested schedule designed to ensure you get the self-care and sleep you need. And that your baby is happy, well fed and also gets the sleep they need. It is a gentle approach focused on flexibility and avoiding tears!

Our website has testimonials from parents who have benefitted from this program, from stay at home, work at home and parents who work out of the home, with a wide variety of careers from celebrity bloggers to working professionals.

Typically the earlier you start the feeding and sleep program the more effective it is, both for smoothly transitioning a baby to sleep through the night and ensuring baby goes to sleep without worrying about tears. Also, that the health practices you teach your baby are carried with them as they continue to grow into toddlers and beyond.

Our gentle baby feeding and sleep program promotes:

- cultivating healthy practices for your baby from birth so that you don't have to try to change established habits later on

- a flexible, predictable feeding and sleep schedule conducive to the lifestyle of busy parents

- ensuring your baby is able to sleep when and where you need them to, in noisy and quiet environments, without sleep props

- effective communication with your baby from birth in order to help you determine their needs and avoid unnecessary tears

- full tummies, lots of snuggle time, and ample rest for families, and

- a practical, efficient and straightforward way of teaching your baby to consistently sleep eight uninterrupted hours each night by the time they are eight weeks old, and a minimum of 10 hours by 12 weeks (3 months old).

The effectiveness of this program is not dependent upon baby's sex or whether baby is the first, second or third born, etc. This program has also been effective for parents with twins. It also does not matter if a baby is bottle fed or breastfed.

This program has been effective for Mothers who have breastfed exclusively, bottle fed (breastmilk/formula) exclusively, and those using a combination of breast and bottle feeding.

Some important benefits of the program and sleep schedule:

- babies consistently sleep eight uninterrupted hours each night by eight weeks, and average between 10 and 12 hours starting at 12 week (but there is a bit of a range as some babies sleep around nine hours; others sleep 12 hours, uninterrupted at three months)

- parents taking a break from, or if baby gets off track of, the schedule can usually transition back to it quickly when they're ready to start again because they've established healthy feeding and sleep practices early on (the only thing baby knows), and

- for those who have used the program consistently, their babies generally go to sleep relaxed on their own and wake up cooing, crying approximately one hour or less in a 24 period.

Babies who have been transitioned to this schedule tend to be content and relatively tear-free because they do not have much to be upset about. The schedule helps ensure that babies are consistently well fed, well rested, and they also have plenty of opportunities for cuddling.

Offering parents a solution to sleep deprivation

We all know that sleep deprivation is not good for us, particularly for prolonged periods of time. Adults require an average of 8.5 hours of sleep each night to report improvements in performance, alertness and mood.[1] Obtaining less than six hours of sleep a night can lead to severe sleep deprivation. Chronic sleep deprivation has many negative impacts on our health including reduced motor and cognitive performance, lower mood, and an imbalance in metabolism and hormones. Fatigue is responsible for 10% of all fatal car accidents behind alcohol (18%) and poor attention (15%).

Lack of sleep is something most parents anticipate when their new baby arrives. A study which tracked the sleep of thousands of men and women with children with growing families showed that sleep for parents hits a low about three months after birth – with the effect strongest in women. The study also found that while parents gradually saw an improvement in their sleep as their firstborn grew, it seems their night-time rest was never quite the same again. It also reported that neither mothers' nor fathers' sleep fully recovers to prepregnancy levels up to six years after the birth of their first child.[2]

It is not realistic to expect eight hours of perfect, uninterrupted sleep with a new baby. However, a gradual improvement in the quality of sleep can be expected as your baby grows, develops, and their need for nutrients at night decreases. This is the basis for our schedule – helping to establish healthy feeding and sleep practices and safely transition babies to a full night of uninterrupted sleep as early as possible (at 12 weeks or three months). We also believe that families thrive when they have a consistent routine that is good for them.

If you are a well-rested Mother (or Father or caregiver) you will be in a much better position to give your baby the care and attention they need while being able to function in your day to day life. Getting enough sleep with an infant and children matters regardless of whether you are a working professional in a corporate environment or if you are stay at home parent, responsible for driving to appointments and taking children to school and activities, not to mention all of your other daily responsibilities.

To us, this represents a positive and worthwhile investment in your health and happiness and your family's, as well as a benefit to society as a whole. Ensuring Mothers have sufficient rest after childbirth is also an integral part of healing.

This program is meant to help lift women up but is also beneficial for any parent with a newborn.

Creating a consistent schedule to avoid sleep training later

Just like an adult, when an infant knows what to expect and is in a routine, anxiety and stress levels can be reduced. When your baby is getting more sleep, you get more sleep! More sleep for baby and Mom reduces the risk of maternal depression and improves your mood and your child's mood.

Up to 30% of children have sleep problems in their first four years which means less sleep for their parents during this time as well. Establishing a sleep routine in infancy may influence sleep patterns as your baby grows up. A study compared newborns on a sleep-training program to a control group followed newborns from birth until six to nine weeks of age. The study found infants on the sleep program had significantly better sleep patterns than the control group. Moreover, the parents in the sleep-program group obtained more uninterrupted sleep, reported less stress generally, and felt more competent when responding to their infants at night compared to the control group.[3]

It can cause unnecessary stress on a Mother and their baby if a newborn is allowed to feed on demand, only to be told months later they should be eating meals at designated times and sleeping through the night.

Our program is an effective option for parents who are interested in balancing the needs of their babies with their own.

Determining the best time to establish a sleep routine for your infant is highly individual, there is no rule for or against when to start. This schedule will not be for everyone – use the aspects of it that resonate with you! We encourage you to review a number of sleep schedules and methods *before* your baby is born until you find a program that you think will work for your family. We suggest doing this before your baby is born because you will be busy when your new baby arrives.

Prior to developing our program, we reviewed a number of approaches to feeding and sleep training.[4] We believe that our program harmonizes your baby's schedule with the family's routine, including eating meals together and sleeping through the night as soon as possible without threatening their physical or emotional wellbeing. And it helps avoid having to sleep train your baby, and as a result, helps avoid tears.

Our goal was to create a program that enables Mothers to have enough time in a day to spend quality time with their babies, in addition to fulfilling their other responsibilities and have some time for themselves. We support a flexible feeding and sleep schedule that allows parents to feed and put their baby or toddler down for a nap within an hour of their desired meal and nap times without having to worry about a meltdown.

We also wanted parents to be able to count on an adequate amount of rest at night themselves in order to function normally during the day, including a full night of sleep (seven or eight uninterrupted hours) as soon as possible after childbirth. This program meets these objectives.

Always consult your healthcare provider to discuss the sleep program you have in mind and to ensure your baby is a good candidate for the sleep program you are considering. Some important circumstances to consider when selecting a program may include low birth weight, weight loss, low immunity, premature birth, or other health concerns your healthcare provider may have.

Baby care basics

Our goal is to help simplify life so you can focus on what matters most to you. We believe in doing what works best for you and your family! Amidst the chaos and fluidity of parenthood, we welcome a touch of certainty, peace of mind and a sense of balance where we can.

There are some predictable things to expect when you have a new baby like dirty diapers and how often they need to feed, all of which we get into in more detail below. Other aspects of it can be less predictable. We're focused on trying to make life as a parent more manageable.

Balancing baby and self care

In the same way that you must put on your own oxygen mask first on an airplane, before helping others, if you take care of yourself you will be in a much better position to care of your baby and everything else. Be honest, you won't be any help to anyone unless you are able to function.

As you may be experiencing first hand right now, feeding a newborn around the clock can be really overwhelming, especially if you're recovering from childbirth and breastfeeding, or if you're doing everything your own. From supplements to secrets for speeding up healing, our Mothers' survival guide for postpartum care is available on our site. A few important things are noted below for parents.

Girlfriend, if you haven't already, let go of the Mommy guilt and the idea you need to be perfect! It doesn't matter what you do, how hard you try or how much you love your baby, the guilt will always be there – when you're making the decision to go back to work or not (and if so, when), to breastfeed or not (and for how long), to take time for yourself (and how much), or to put your baby down or let them cry (and for how long).

As a new Mom, expect your hormones and sense of balance to be out of whack for a while. Familiarize yourself and your loved ones with the signs and symptoms of baby blues and postpartum depression (PPD).

Baby blues and PPD are real, serious, and important to address. Read more about this on our site and discuss it with your healthcare provider.

Leaning on your support network is also important for new parents. Have at least one friend or family member that you know you can call for support at any hour of the day or night. You may also find it helpful and therapeutic to keep a journal to document your observations. Include how you are feeling and how you are coping with having a new baby.

The sooner your baby is on a schedule that works for you, the sooner you and your family will benefit from more predictability and rest.
Establishing healthy practices for your baby from the moment they are born is important so that it's the only thing baby will know. You won't have to try to change established habits later on. This makes things easier for everyone in the family, especially if you want to avoid tears.

Your baby's sleep cycle

A newborn baby sleeps between 11 to 17 hours in a 24 hour period. The average is around 14 hours, usually in one to four hour blocks at first. Newborns spend more time in REM sleep which is important for their brain development. Dr. Pam has posts on our website which provide more detailed information about this if you're interested.

What this means is that newborns need to be fed breast milk or formula at least eight times every 24 hours. In other words, they will feed once every three to four hours around the clock. Some newborns may even need to feed as often as every two hours, especially if there are health concerns, if your baby is not getting enough at feeding time, or if your healthcare provider recommends feeding more frequently.

Over time, your baby should begin to sleep more at night than during the day. Some infants can achieve eight to 12 hours of uninterrupted sleep as early as six weeks of age. But this will all depend on the unique characteristics of your baby and their doctor's recommendations, as well as your baby's environment and the feeding schedule you use.

Tracking your baby's sleep cycle on their chart from day one

The fact is, you need to feed a newborn baby every two to four hours, which is at least eight times every 24 hours. Since life with a newborn tends to be a blur, we recommend tracking your baby's feeding and sleep cycle on the chart we've provided from day one. Over time, you might prefer to consistently feed your baby once every three hours around the clock instead of randomly every two to four hours.

Your baby's chart is an easy reference guide for you and any other of their caregivers. The chart can be used until your baby is a year or older, with as little or as much detail as you would like. Let their other caregivers know about the schedule you are using and have them fill in your baby's chart so they can help you establish consistency.

Chances are, your baby's healthcare provider has probably asked you to track certain things about your new baby anyway. For example, how many minutes your baby is breastfeeding for or how many ounces they drink out of a bottle, temperature, and how many wet and dirty diapers they have in 24 hours. Other things include tracking daily medication, and vitamin D intake if your baby is drinking breast milk. In the *comments* section of the chart you can also write down general observations about your baby. For example, if your baby isn't feeling well or is teething, they may be a bit fussy. Other things to note are dates of healthcare provider appointments, and baby's immunization appointments and any adverse reactions they have, such as fever, etc.

As time goes on, you may find it helpful to note feeding and sleep patterns (for example, if baby has larger feedings at every second feeding throughout the day and at night), and times when your baby tends to be more fussy (late afternoon or early evening etc.). When you introduce solids, consider documenting the introduction of each new type of food, noting any reactions your baby is having. Once your baby is consistently sleeping through the night, it may make sense to reduce the level of detail in their chart to only monitoring feeding and sleep.

Why a schedule with a newborn is worth it

For the first few weeks after delivery, expect to be in survival mode, healing and exhausted from childbirth, sleep deprived, and stressed about being a new parent. It can be so much more difficult if you're suffering from baby blues or PPD. The sooner you can avoid sleep deprivation the better it will be for you, your new baby, and your family. This assumes of course that you value sleep for you and your family.

This program is meant to help make your life easier with a new baby. The earlier you start a consistent schedule after delivery, the quicker and easier it will be to transition your baby to your desired schedule. Although we recommend being firm and consistent, we urge you to balance this with patience and gentleness for you and baby. In the same way that certain babies walk and talk earlier than others, some babies may take longer than others to adapt to a desired schedule.

Absent health concerns, doing this work up front really does help simplify life. It can save your family from a lot of unnecessary stress, energy and tears as your baby gets older, by avoiding sleep training and having to break habits! Habits can develop for babies in as little as a few days (i.e., things like skipping naps regularly during the day, delayed feedings and late bedtime, and baby becoming accustomed to falling asleep on an adult, being rocked to sleep or in a baby swing, etc.). What you teach your baby will depend on your preferences – and will begin to come naturally and should stick with them as they continue to grow.

Once you have established a consistent feeding and sleep schedule, expect more predictability in life.

If you are using the schedule below, you should find that things become much more flexible in a matter of a few months, to the point of being able to feed within an hour of the feeding time you designate based on your baby's chart. You may also find that it is not a big deal to skip or adjust the time of a nap during the day. You should also find that it is not difficult to switch to a new time zone within four or so hours of your normal time zone.

Communicating with your baby

Learning how to effectively communicate with your baby is essential to helping understand their needs, keep them content, and soothe them when they are upset. There are also a handful of important checks to do throughout the day (and night) to help with this.

How to effectively communicate with your baby

Over time you will get to know your baby's personality but when it comes to communicating with your newborn baby, the Dunstan Baby Language provides a life changing approach to preventing tears. In short, according to this baby language, the five universal words or *sound reflexes* used by infants are:

Eairh – baby has gas,
Eh – baby needs to burp,
Heh – baby is physically uncomfortable,
Neh – baby is hungry, and
Owh – baby is tired.

Check out Priscilla Dunstan's interview with Oprah at dunstanbaby.com. It's relatively quick to learn, especially as you get to know your baby more (and there's an app available).

It can be fun trying to figure out their needs and wants in between raspberries, giggles and coos. But for times that you just want to cut to the chase, consider teaching them baby sign language. Baby sign can be really helpful when your baby is old enough to eat solids. Start with common words like *hungry, thirsty, more, finished, sleep time,* and *I love you*. Other helpful signs are *play time, please, thank you* and *excuse me*.

Babies pick up on things very quickly, and they love listening to you sing and talk. Tell your baby what time it is so that they understand what is going on. In no time at all, they will know and understand when it's bath time, nap time, play time, bedtime, breakfast, lunch and dinner.

This may sound silly but to help develop your baby's ability to communicate verbally, consider speaking with them like they are a person. Try to avoid baby talk and use correct grammar and pronunciation when speaking.

You may also want to consider teaching good manners by demonstrating appropriate etiquette. For example, using please and thank you. Other things may be sitting politely at the dinner table, not playing with or throwing food, and not allowing toys and electronic devices at the table. Many of these things depend on your preferences.

Doing all the important checks throughout the day and at night

There is a lot to be said for being proactive rather than reactive to your baby especially before putting them down to sleep.

The main things to check for, especially when your baby is starting to fuss, are to make sure that they are well-fed, they are burped, and they are comfortable, meaning they have a clean diaper and that they are not too hot or cold.

Keep in mind that babies also tend to fuss if they are overtired, or if they are sick or teething.

Diaper rash is also something to keep an eye out for. It can come on quickly and fiercely! We recommend putting a type of diaper rash cream or balm on your baby's bum each time you change them to help prevent diaper rash. At minimum you will want to do this until your newborn's poop changes from being sticky and greenish-black in colour to brown and batter-like in consistency – expect it to take a few poops, or a day or two, before you notice a change in colour and consistency.

You can read more about your baby's wet and dirty diapers in the *Healthy feeding practices* section below. If your baby has a diaper rash, start with increased airtime or diaper-free time. When you put your baby's diaper back on, be sure to apply diaper rash cream.

There are many natural alternatives to petroleum laced baby creams, gels and balms that can also work well for treating cradle cap or dry skin on children and adults. We like products that are clean and fresh, and avoid irritation, especially for sensitive skin. Some of the baby and household products we like can be found in the product reviews on our site. Never hesitate to reach out to ask us for product recommendations!

Healthy feeding and sleep practices and more

Quick reference guide for baby feeding and sleep

Healthy feeding practices — 19

Your newborn: eating, sleeping and pooping — 19
How to tell when baby is hungry — 20
A full tummy (or whole feeding) at each feeding — 21
The bedtime top up feeding — 22
1.5 hour feeding windows every 3 hours — 23
How to tell when baby's tummy is full — 24
Signs your baby is not getting enough — 26
Guideline amounts for breast and bottle feeding — 27

Breastfeeding and bottle feeding — 29
Nipple confusion — 29
Must have products — 30
Your breasts postpartum — 32
Increasing milk supply — 33
What not to eat — 34
Expressing (pumping) — 35
Breastmilk storage — 36
Formula feeding — 36

Introducing solid foods — 37
Allergies and food sensitivities — 38
Introducing solid foods — 39
Hypoallergenic food introduction chart — 40
Higher risk foods — 40
Dealing with picky eaters — 41
The importance of iron from six months onward — 41
Must haves for baby's solid foods — 41
Ingredients in your baby's food — 42
How to make your own baby food (if you want to) — 42

Healthy feeding practices 44

Reducing the risk of SIDS 44

Invest in a baby monitor 44

How long to let your baby cry for 45

Teaching baby to be patient 45

Swaddling until ready to transition to a sleep sack 45

Putting baby to sleep in their crib while awake 46

Avoiding dependence on sleep props 47

Teaching baby to fall asleep in any environment 47

Avoiding an overtired baby 48

The value of quiet time 48

Helpful homeopathic remedies for sleep, etc. 49

Tips when travelling with baby 50

Tips specific to your baby's schedule 51
 Feeding every three hours with a nap in between 51
 Waking between feedings or at night 51
 Stirring in the morning 51
 Getting off track and then back on again 52

Know how to soothe your baby 53

Healthy feeding practices

Your newborn: eating, sleeping and pooping

Newborn babies can sleep 14 or more hours in a 24 hour period. Your baby will most likely be feeding every two to four hours in the beginning so you will feed your newborn baby at least 8 times in 24 hours.

Generally, a newborn's stomach is the size of a cherry the first two days of life, a whole walnut by day four, and finally around the size of an egg at two weeks of age. Typically, a newborn will consume two to three ounces per feed in the first month.

Your newborn baby should have approximately six wet diapers per day by the first two weeks if they are getting enough to drink. Within the first two days of life, your baby should have minimum one or two wet and one or two solid or poopy diapers. The stool colour will mostly be dark green to black (this is referred to as meconium). During the next two days you should see at least three or four wet diapers and at least three poopy diapers.

From one to three weeks of age expect five or six heavy wet diapers with yellow or clear urine and three to five poops per day. As your baby's digestive system develops the stool consistency, colour, and frequency changes as well.

After five weeks their bowel movements will be less frequent but larger. These guidelines are for both breastfed and formula fed babies. If your baby is having less frequent bowel movements it is most likely normal; however, have a conversation with your healthcare provider.

Contact your healthcare provider if your baby goes more than six hours without a wet diaper.

How to tell when baby is hungry

Your baby will tell you if they're hungry, you just need to watch for the signs! As you get to know your baby, you will learn to recognize when they are hungry, and distinguish their hunger signs from other mannerisms. For example, some babies will suck on their fingers, thumbs or soothers regardless of whether or not they are hungry.

In addition to recognizing the sound reflexes outlined by the Dunstan Baby Language (*Neh* sound means baby is hungry), there are other ways to tell if your baby is hungry.

Early signs your baby is hungry may include lip smacking, opening their mouth, sticking out their tongue, and sucking on pretty much anything they can get their mouth on.

As babies get hungrier, they may also begin bang on your shoulders and chest, or move their head from side to side. If your baby is breastfed, they will probably nuzzle around the chest of the person that is holding them, particularly if that person has breasts. If you move your finger across the cheek of a hungry baby, they will follow your finger in the direction you move it while opening their mouth (their rooting reflex).

If you miss the initial hunger signs, your baby will likely get restless or frantic and start to cry. If your newborn gets to the point where they are crying hysterically, they may end up tiring themselves out and fall asleep shortly after (either before or half way through a feeding) and wake up within the following hour or so for another feeding.

This pattern of constant feeding is not ideal unless you prefer to or are okay with constantly demand feeding your baby rather than putting your baby on a schedule that works for you and your family. It is all about personal preference and what works for you!

A full tummy (or whole feeding) at each feeding

It can take up to 1.5 hours, sometimes even two hours, from the time you start feeding a newborn until they are ready for a nap. We are distinguishing here between your baby falling in and out of sleep on you during feeding time compared to a real that nap that is between 1.5 to 2.5 hours long. Either way, you will be able to see your baby's patterns on their chart once you start tracking their feeding and sleep.

You may find that your baby may be prone to falling asleep more often during a feeding or is less alert for at least a few weeks following delivery especially if they were born premature. Consult with your baby's healthcare provider if you are finding it difficult to wake your baby to make sure there is nothing medically wrong.

Because it can take so long to feed your baby each time, your feedings can start blending together resulting in constant feeding around the clock with no real breaks. Also, if your baby is not full between feedings, you run the risk of them regularly waking up every hour or less for another feeding. Not only is this exhausting, it leaves very little time in between to handle other responsibilities and rest!

To help begin to distinguish between feeding time and nap time, try to establish a clear half an hour to a maximum 1.5 hour feeding window each time your feed your baby. Be sure that your baby has a full tummy (or whole feeding) before you stop feeding them before their nap. There are a few other things you can do like swaddle or put a sleepsack on at nap time, which are mentioned in the schedule below, but this is key.

If you know your baby has had enough prior to the end of the 1.5 hour mark, after half an hour or an hour for example, great – stop feeding. Until you are sure your baby has a full tummy, try to top up every 15 minutes during each 1.5 hour feeding window – repeating the top up helps parents get a gage for how much their baby really needs. There is almost no better opportunity for you to snuggle, take a quick nap on you, or play with your baby, while periodically trying to top them up. At the end of the 1.5 hour feeding window, if you are still not sure if your baby has had enough, you have a final top up opportunity before putting them down for their nap or bedtime (this extra feeding opportunity is why we feel more frequent feedings work with our schedule).

Gentle ways to wake your baby include rubbing the bottom of their feet or touching their feet or other bare skin with a cool facecloth. Removing extra layers of clothing or undressing your baby can be effective as well.

If you try topping your baby up after the 1.5 hour mark, you risk of running into blurring the lines with the next feeding window.

The bedtime top up feeding

The bedtime top up feeding is really important when your baby starts to sleep longer at night. This feeding is the only exception to the recommendation to feed within a 1.5 hour feeding window because we consider part of the feeding at dinnertime (i.e., around 6:00 p.m.).

The reason for this exception is that the top up feeding may start an hour or more after you start the dinnertime feeding. To help your baby sleep for extended periods at night, you sort of treat the bedtime bottle like it is its own feeding from the time your baby is three months old until they are a year old. Depending on how much baby has had for dinner, the bedtime bottle may contain slightly less or more breastmilk or formula compared to the other bottles fed in the 24 hour period.

To explain why we consider the top up as part of the dinnertime feeding, even though we're jumping ahead bit, we suggest starting to phase the bedtime top up bottle out completely anytime after 13 months to help facilitate potty training. When your baby is older, this may turn into a snack of some sort instead which we discuss in more detail below.

Read more about bedtime tops up in Week 12 of the schedule below.

1.5 hour feeding windows every 3 hours

Your healthcare provider may recommend feeding your newborn more frequently than every three hours (8 times in 24 hours). This could be due to health concerns like blood glucose issues, dehydration, jaundice, or to make sure baby is gaining enough weight. Other reasons could be that your baby is not getting enough milk (not latching properly if breastfeeding) or that your baby is going through a growth spurt.
Feeding more frequently, or even demand feeding, could also be a personal preference which is okay too as long as it works for you.

If you prefer to feed once every three hours but need to feed more often temporarily, our schedule is conducive to these more frequent feedings. This is because we recommend 1.5 hour feeding windows at first. You can feed your baby a whole feeding at the beginning and end of what would normally be a 1.5 hour feeding window. So you would feed every 1.5 to two hours with your baby having shorter naps in between.

Making sure that your baby always has a full tummy at the end of each feeding is important because it will help you eventually set up a schedule where they feed every three hours rather than more frequently. For best results, work toward establishing feeding windows once every three hours around the clock (8 whole feedings in 24 hours).

This will make more sense after you've reviewed the schedule below and designate the feeding times on your baby's chart. But essentially, you start feeding your baby within a half an hour of their designated feeding time you circle on their chart. From the time you start feeding them, feed for up to 1.5 hours until they have a full tummy.

There are a few important tips to help smoothly transition your baby to feeding once every three hours rather than more frequently. First, be intentional about when you start the transition to feeding every three hours. Start the transition at a feeding when you think your baby will drink a fair amount to fill their tummy before going down for 1.5 to 2.5 hour nap afterward. This is especially important if you find that they eat more at some feedings than others. Your baby may tend to drink more at the 6:00 a.m. breakfast, noon lunch and 6:00 p.m. dinner/bedtime top up feedings and slightly less in between feedings, especially if they are 12 weeks old and sleeping 10-12 hours uninterrupted at night.

Also consider waiting until baby has just had a small prior feeding, or baby is waking from a long nap and hasn't been feeding for at least two hours. Try to start as close as possible to one of the feeding times you circled on baby's feeding chart (i.e., within half an hour of that specific feeding time). If you're using our schedule, you will probably be feeding every three hours starting at either 6:00 a.m. or 7:00 a.m. for breakfast. If possible, consider starting the transition at breakfast one morning.

How to tell when baby's tummy is full

Over time, you should be able to identify patterns in respect of how much your baby eats at certain times of the day and every 24 hours. For example, they may eat less before they have a poop, have really big breakfasts and bedtime feedings, or alternate between large and small feedings. Looking back on their chart can help you going forward, especially if you get off track for a few days.

As your baby gets older, it will become more obvious when they have had a whole feeding. Signs that a baby has a full tummy include slowing down during a feeding and seeming uninterested, closing their mouth, turning their head away, pushing their head away from your breast or bottle, or falling asleep during a feeding. Falling asleep during a feeding may not be a reliable indicator that your newborn is full because it is very common for newborns to fall asleep during feeding.

After six months, your baby may tell you they are full in baby sign or another obvious mannerism. They will also be prone to getting more distracted and may seem less interested in feeding with all of the fun sights and sounds around them. But they may not necessarily be full at this point so it's always a good idea to double check by topping up.

Waking up in the middle of nap time

If your baby is continually waking up for a whole feeding again within an hour and a half of you putting them down for a nap, they may not be getting enough at their feedings. This could possibly be due to lack of milk production or a poor latch. Nursing difficulties could be caused by a tongue tie, or tensions and restrictions in a baby's head, spine or body. See below for more information about breastfeeding.

If your baby is consistently waking up to feed in the middle of a nap, they may not be filling their tummy at feeding time. Try to make sure each feeding results in your baby having a full tummy. This is because you want to help avoid getting into the habit of having to give your baby many partial feedings throughout the day on a demand basis resulting in no flexibility or predictability. After they are done, put them down again to finish their nap and push the next feeding back accordingly.

Simply adjust feeding and sleep times throughout the rest of the day to get back on track with your desired schedule.

Rule: always feed a hungry baby

Letting babies cry themselves to sleep, especially when they are hungry, will not benefit anyone. If your baby wakes up to feed 45 minutes into a nap and has another whole feeding, they may be going through a growth spurt. Growth spurts are common especially around three weeks six weeks, and three months.

If your baby is going through a growth spurt it may cause a change in their eating and sleeping patterns. Babies also become more efficient in removing milk from the breast as they grow which may result in a shorter feeding time. These are all normal activities however some parents think these changes may mean their baby is ready for solids which is not always the case.

Make sure you are keeping in contact with your healthcare provider to track growth changes at least every two months for the first year.

Signs your baby is not getting enough

A baby's weight and growth history is generally a good indicator of whether they are drinking enough. It is normal for babies to lose up to 7% of their birth weight in the first few days of life. They should return to this weight or surpass it by the second week mark – after this time most breastfed babies gain around 170g (60 ounces) per week.

If you are concerned that your baby is not growing or gaining weight, contact your healthcare provider and make sure you are keeping up with your infant milestone examinations. Some health clinics allow parents to drop in without an appointment to weigh their baby, or you could always buy a scale if you prefer. Keeping track of weight gain or loss in the *comments* section of your baby's chart for peace of mind.

Don't worry if your baby does not quite have as much as you think they should at a feeding. Like you, they will have more or less to eat or drink depending on how they feel. Your baby may eat less if they are not feeling well due to teething, being overtired or if they aren't feeling well.

General signs that your baby is not getting enough fluids or is dehydrated include, if:

- fontanels (soft spots on their head) and eyes are sunken
- baby is crying but no tears are produced
- baby has dry or brittle hair and/or skin
- baby is lethargic, and/or
- baby has gone more than six hours without a wet diaper.

Contact your healthcare provider immediately if your baby is showing any of these signs.

Guideline amounts for breast and bottle feeding

Below is a general guideline for the number of ounces a baby should have in 24 hours. The number of feedings corresponds with our schedule below by phase.

Weeks 1-2

- 8 feedings in 24 hours (approx. once every 3 hours)
- 2-3 ounces (60-90 ml) per feeding
- Total of 12-30 ounces (360-900 ml) in 24 hours

Weeks 3-7

- 7 feedings in 24 hours
- 3-4 ounces (90-120 ml) per feeding
- Total of 18-32 ounces (540-960 ml) in 24 hours

Weeks 8-11

- 6 feedings in 24 hours
- 4-6 ounces (120-180 ml) per feeding
- 20-36 ounces (600-1080 ml) in 24 hours

Week 12

- 5 feedings in 24 hours
- 4-6 ounces (120-180 ml) per feeding
- 20-36 ounces (600-1080 ml) in 24 hours

4-7 months

- 5 feedings in 24 hours
- 5-6 ounces (150-180 ml) per feeding
- 25-36 ounces (750-1080 ml) in 24 hours

7-12 months

- 5 feedings in 24 hours
- 6-8 ounces (180-240 ml) per feeding
- 18-32 ounces (900-1,200 ml) in 24 hours

There are few things to note when reading this chart, especially if you are planning to use the baby feeding and sleep schedule below.

There is no set number of minutes that your baby will breast- feed before they are full. You could try to breastfeed your baby for 15 to 20 minutes on each breast at first and then it's a bit of trial and error from there! Likewise, there are no predetermined number of ounces (or bites of baby food) that your baby will have.

These are general guidelines and this will not be the same for every baby so your baby's chart will be important. As a new- born, your baby may only breastfeed for 10 minutes on each breast or drink one to three ounces, etc.

There will be times when your baby needs an extra feeding in a 24 hour period. This may be due to a growth spurt or because they did not have enough to eat during the previous day due to a cold or teething, etc. Always feed your baby when they are hungry.

This chart does not refer to the bedtime top up feeding be- cause we technically consider it to be part of the dinner feeding (and it may be dropped completely when baby is a toddler if they do not have a bedtime snack).

Never microwave formula or breastmilk. Always throw out the remaining formula when baby is finished – never reheat formula!

At the four to six month mark, consult with your baby's healthcare provider about introducing solids. More on this below as well.

There may be one to 1.5 hours between the time you start to feed your baby their dinner and their bedtime feeding, especially if you move dinnertime to an earlier time one evening or just generally. If so and you bottle feed, you may want to make a fresh bottle before bed (baby formula tends to only be good for an hour – always read the instructions on the container to make sure).

Breastfeeding and bottle feeding

The decision to breastfeed your baby versus feeding expressed breastmilk or formula during the early part their life is, unfortunately, a controversial topic. We understand that there are a number of reasons why women do not feed their babies breastmilk, including personal preference, for health reasons or lack of supply. We acknowledge those realities and respect their decisions.

There is no denying that there are a number of health benefits associated with feeding your baby breastmilk. Breastmilk is a whole food that is dynamic and changes with the needs of the infant as they grow. It contains vitamins, nutrients and antibodies, including essential fatty acids important for brain development. Unfortunately, there is nothing on the market that is comparable and scientists are not able to completely replicate the qualities found in breastmilk.

If you have chosen breastfeeding, consider having some formula of your choice readily available just in case it takes longer than expected for your milk to come in or if you don't produce enough. Check our site for our favourite products, including best formula and other baby products.

Nipple confusion

The need to suck is an innate way for a baby to feel calm and relaxed. Some babies even suck their thumbs in the womb! This need is stronger in some infants more than others. Our program is conducive to exclusively breastfeeding, exclusively bottle feeding (expressed milk or formula) or a mix of something in between. See our FAQ's for more info.

We think it is nice for other family members to help feed and bond with your baby, and for Mom to have a break. However, some girlfriends swear that their babies refuse to drink from anything but their breast.

Another thing to keep in mind, particularly in the early weeks of breastfeeding, is the importance for a newborn to first learn how to attach to their Mothers nipple to ensure proper latching, stronger suction, and reduce chances of sore nipples.

Introducing a pacifier or bottle too early can, on occasion, confuse the newborn as there is a difference between the two and how the mouth is orientated. If breastfeeding is not an option or if milk flow doesn't come in and supplementing is required, most infants will adapt but it may be beneficial to discuss with a lactation consultant.

Must have products

There are a number of products available to help make breastfeeding, expressing milk and bottle feeding easier, all listed below. Our site contains specific brand and product recommendations for products we have used and believe in.

- If you are expressing, rent a hospital grade breast pump or invest in a top of the line product (because, obviously, these are your breasts). Sometimes employee insurance coverage packages cover some or all of the cost of pumps if medically prescribed. A hands-free pump will give you the ability to be mobile while you are pumping, whether you are pumping in your office at work or doing chores at home.

- Invest in comfortable and supportive nursing bras.

- If you are more comfortable covering up while nursing or expressing milk, consider picking up nursing cover. We like the nursing covers that provide coverage while enabling your to see your baby nursing with it on.

- Use nursing pads because leaks are embarrassing. We have found that reusable bamboo pads are more discrete than the cotton and disposable pads.

- Invest in a feeding pillow. They are so helpful for breastfeeding, and also offer great support while bottle feeding.

- There are a diverse line of products related to breastfeeding and pumping, including bottles, freezer bags and breast shields. Breastmilk can also be frozen using ice cube trays.

- Always have nipple cream handy. Note that placenta salve also works well for sore nipples (just throwing this out there for you to think about and will discuss placenta products below).

- Choose your baby bottles carefully! There are so many bottles available on the market that it can be overwhelming. Here are some considerations we think are important. First, we prefer to use glass bottles because we don't necessarily trust plastic even if is BPA and PVC free. Second, we like brands that offer a variety of nipple flows to choose from, including quicker flows as your baby gets older, or if you need a larger Y nipple if the formula you are using is thicker than what your baby is used to. Some brands even sell sippy cup nipples to put on their bottles for when it's time to transition your baby. Last but certainly not least, do the research on the venting system of the bottle you have selected. We prefer bottles that are clinically designed to reduce colic and gas.

- Don't forget to pick up a few bottle cleaners. Some even stand up on their own.

- Pick up convenient sterilizing equipment. If you are sterilizing your baby bottles and equipment and are unable to boil them (because you are travelling or just because it's a hassle sometimes), there are microwaveable options as well as countertop sterilizers. There are even microwaveable bags for sterilizing breast pump, bottles and equipment on the go.

- If you are bottle feeding, purchase a bottle warmer (it may sound excessive, but they are truly amazing).

Your breasts postpartum

Your breasts may feel hot, swollen and tender after you've had a baby. For the first few days, your breasts will likely be soft because they only contain colostrum, a thick and sticky yellow to orange coloured milk containing nutrients and antibodies that will help to protect your baby from infection.

If you choose to breastfeed your baby, we hope that you are one of the lucky ones whose babies latch perfectly without any effort and that you produce a ton of milk. If not, know you are not alone! If you can, hang in there and know that it usually tends to get better over time. If not, it is what it is, let it go (guilt free!).

In addition to the health benefits for your baby, breastfeeding can be a great bonding experience. (Skin on skin contact with parents is beneficial for babies regardless of whether they are being breastfed or not.) Breastfeeding also helps your uterus contract after delivery, and burns a lot of calories, if that's a priority for you. However, breastfeeding often hurts and is uncomfortable at first. It can also take a while for you and your baby to get the hang of (like six week or more sometimes!).

Also important to know, it usually takes three or four days after delivery for milk to come in. Colostrum is very difficult to pump out. Your healthcare provider may recommend you manually express it and feed baby with a syringe (or cup or spoon) until your milk comes in.

Expressing breastmilk (or pumping) can be extra work. Although you may have a bit more control over your breasts when you pump, it is time consuming, especially cleaning pump paraphernalia and bottles.

For assistance with milk supply and latching, or if you are experiencing pain while breastfeeding (you may have thrush or other issues), consult your healthcare provider who should be able to recommend a lactation consultant and other resources like La Leche League (lllc.ca).

Increasing milk supply

A food or substance that is known to improve milk production and flow is referred to as a galactogogue. Foods known to increase milk supply:

- oats
- nuts/seeds (esp. ground flaxseeds, pumpkin seeds, walnuts)
- dates (palm dates
- brewer's yeast and hops (historically Guinness beer was recommended... not so much a recommendation now!), and
- the herbs: fenugreek, blessed thistle, and fennel.

There are a number of nursing teas on the market to help with milk production which contain some of these herbs, as well as just plain fenugreek herbal tea.

Foods that may contribute to low supply:

- caffeine (sorry to say tired Mama!)
- the herb sage, and
- some sources say pineapples.

Refer to the posts on our site relating to foods helping to increase to help milk supply. Also try our lactation cookie recipe!

There is also prescription medication for assisting with milk production but your qualified Naturopathic Doctor (Naturopath) should be able to advise on the appropriate product for you. Feel free to contact us if you are having trouble finding a suitable Naturopath in your area, we may be able to provide a referral.

What not to eat

Unless you have a known food sensitivity or allergy, it is ideal to have a variety of healthy foods and not avoid certain foods to prevent allergies in your baby.

A study found that Mothers who consumed tree nuts and peanuts five times per week had the lowest risk of their child developing allergies to nuts compared to Mothers who did not. This shows that when exposed in-utero, infants develop a strong immune system to detect what is safe and what is food versus an allergen.[5] Do not consume tree nuts if you as the Mother have an allergy!

There is also clinical evidence that Moms who had a varied diet with lots of flavours and spices had more adventurous eaters when their child was older.

You may find it helpful to avoid certain foods that are known to cause gas or discomfort for your baby, including high allergen foods that can cause reactions such as rashes. These may include spicy foods, dairy products, citrus fruits, tomatoes, eggs, wheat, fish, soy and peanut products. Honey is not safe for nursing Mothers or infants under the age of one.

Consult with your healthcare provider prior to consuming alcohol as well as recreational and prescribed medications. See the post on our site about medications that are safe while breastfeeding.

Colic, gas, burping and probiotics

Always ensure that your baby is well-burped during and after feeding. There are also baby bottles that are clinically designed to reduce colic and gas. Tummy rubs and moving their legs up into their abdomen can also be helpful.

There are many good quality infant probiotics on the market that can help settle an upset stomach which also provide many further health benefits (find out more here). Consult with your healthcare provider prior to giving your infant anything by mouth to help with gas; especially if they are under six months of age.

Expressing (pumping)

Expressing milk is not always the easiest process. Consistent breastfeeding and pumping practices each day, and slow transitions when makes changes, can make breastfeeding much easier and much more comfortable. A few key considerations are below.

- If you plan to breastfeed and pump, always breastfeed first so that you don't risk running out when baby is feeding.

- In terms of frequency, it's not the same for everyone. A general recommendation is to pump more frequently to help ensure production (every 3 hours for about 10 minutes per breast).

- However, if you don't have any concerns with milk supply, you may find that you produce the same amount of milk in a 24 hour period when you pump less often for slightly longer periods of time (i.e., once every four, six or even eight hours for 20 or 30 minutes per breast).

- Monitor how much you are pumping at night, because you don't want to be in a position where you need to wake up to pump every few hours even though your baby is sleeping through the night. However, if you have concerns regarding your milk supply you probably won't want to wait longer than eight hours between breastfeeding or pumping. Plus your breasts may be so full! You will find the right balance for you.

- Although one of your breasts might produce more milk than the other, it helps to try to keep things equal. This is mostly because engorgement and blocked milk ducts really hurt. Try to breastfeed and pump for the same number of minutes on each breast each time. You can keep track of this with a stopwatch – there's probably one on your pump as well as your cell phone. Also, if you start feeding your baby on your right breast for one feeding, start on the left at the next feeding and so on. This is easy to keep track of on your baby's chart.

- Always make sure that you are on top of engorgement and blockage issues. Placing cold compresses on your breasts will tend to help reduce milk flow whereas warm compresses will help to increase it. In addition to putting a warm facecloth on your breasts or having a warm shower or bath, massaging your breasts and gently moving your hand from the outside of your breast toward the areola may make them feel better if you have a blockage or lump between feedings or pumping sessions.

- Making sure to taper down slowly when you decide to cut back or stop pumping or breastfeeding altogether. We recommend shortening your pumping time by two or three minutes each day until you are at zero minutes. Regardless of whether you are increasing or decreasing the number of minutes you are pumping, have breast pads handy for leaking.

Breastmilk storage

Breastmilk is like liquid gold, so you won't want any to go to waste unless it is necessary for the health of your baby. Things to consider and consult with your healthcare provider about are below.

- Freshly breastmilk is good for up to four hours at room temperature. Use within five to seven days stored in the fridge.

- If you are freezing breastmilk, do so immediately after it has been pumped. Frozen breastmilk that is being stored in a deep freeze should be used within six months of the initial storage date, and within three months if stored in a refrigerator freezer.

- Always thaw breastmilk in fridge. If breastmilk was previously frozen, use within 24 hours from the time it is thawed.

- Never heat breastmilk in a microwave because it changes the properties in it. If you do not have a bottle warmer, place the bag or bottle of milk in a bowl or cup of hot water to warm.

- You can reheat fresh breastmilk once only. Never reheat or refreeze breastmilk that has previously been frozen.

Formula feeding

Your healthcare provider can help you select an appropriate formula based on your baby's needs. We prefer organic brands of formula that we can read and understand the list of ingredients for (see our site for specific product recommendations). A favourite homemade rice milk based recipe of ours is from Dr. Beverly Huang at Grassroots Naturopathic Medicine Health Clinic (grassrootsnaturopathic.com).

It's never a bad idea to mix formula with water that has been filtered and boiled unless you don't need to add water, according to the instructions.

When transitioning your baby from breastfeeding to a bottle or sippy cup, consider leaving them with your partner, family member or caregiver for the day or a weekend – this way your baby won't be able to insist Mom feeds them (unless of course Mom only feeding is what works best for your family).

When transitioning your baby from breastmilk to formula, start by mixing the two in a bottle. Begin with ¾ breastmilk and ¼ formula, then go down to ½ and ½, followed by ¼ breastmilk and ¾ formula and so on.

Always throw away the leftover portion – never reheat!

Introducing solid foods

The introduction of solids is generally recommended between four and six months but you should always consult with your healthcare provider first. Signs that indicate your baby may be ready for solids include:

- teeth coming in

- ability to sit up independently and support their head

- ability to grab food and pick up small objects

- showing strong interest in food (watching others eat, etc.)

- tongue extrusion reflex is fading – the first four months, tongue thrust reflex prevents infants from choking on foreign objects and causes them to push food out of their mouths, and

- ability to prepare food in their mouth before swallowing – prior to four months, a baby's swallowing mechanism is designed to work with sucking but not chewing – between four and six months, most infants develop the ability to move food from the front of the mouth to the back instead of letting it wallow around in the mouth and get spit out.

Babies will drink less when they begin to eat more solids so you may want to keep track of solid and liquid intake in your baby's chart until the one year mark.

For consistency, from the time you start feeding solids to the eight or 10 month mark, consider feeding solids at breakfast, lunch and dinner times only – solids first then liquids. Feed breastmilk or formula at each feeding even though baby may drink less at breakfast, lunch and dinner times because they are more full from solids. After the eight (or 10) month mark, add solids at snack times.

Allergies and food sensitivities

Depending on the healthcare provider consulted, the suggested timing and order for introducing certain foods to your baby could vary significantly. If there is a history of food sensitivity reactions in a family member (parent or sibling) such as eczema or asthma, your healthcare provider may recommend that certain foods be introduced slower.

An anaphylactic allergy occurs when the body reactions to a substance mediated by IgE antibodies to produce histamine and is a medical emergency. With subsequent exposure to the reactive substance, the body mounts a stronger response each time making them quite dangerous after the initial attack. A sensitivity on the other hand is a delayed IgG mediated response which makes the suspect food a bit more challenging to identify. And just to confuse things more there are food intolerances! Intolerances do not involve the immune system at all but cause irritation in the digestive system, which can lead to gas and bloating or diarrhea and constipation.

A true allergic reaction generally follows the same symptom picture no matter if from food or from something in the environment. Signs to watch for include red patches or welts on the skin, swelling or itchy lips or eyes, runny nose, fatigue, and difficulty breathing.

80-90% of children with true food allergies are allergic to one or more of the following: dairy, eggs, peanuts and other tree nuts, shellfish, soy, and wheat. Food sensitivities can be triggered by the same list but can also be from a variety of other sources.

Most sensitivities do not show up in obvious ways until a few days after ingestion so even if your baby initially did well on a food, continue monitoring them.

Cooking the majority of your baby's first foods can reduce the risk of allergy development.

In the case of an allergy, the first exposure is usually a mild reaction; however, with subsequent expose, there is a high chance of a more dramatic reaction so care is needed when trying that food again. Then waiting two months and do not introduce anything new until the symptoms clear up.

If your child is developing seasonal or environmental allergies, they most likely will have more nasal congestion which could resemble a cold. There is a chart available on our site for helping to distinguish between a cold, flu, and allergies.

Introducing new foods

When starting new foods with your infant or child, monitoring for food allergies is important. If they shows signs of having an allergy or sensitivity, it can be easier to determine what is causing the issue if you've been introducing new foods one by one.

Keep track of each new food introduction and any reactions on your baby's chart.

If you are concerned about a food allergy or sensitivity, one way to slowly introduce a food is to place it on their cheek away from their mouths for 10-20 minutes to see if any red- ness or swelling develops. After this, wait 12-24 hours and monitor for symptoms. If none occur, then can try a small amount of their lips and again monitor for symptoms. This is a good strategy for first introduction of common food allergies such as peanuts.

Below is a hypoallergenic food introduction chart. Consult with your healthcare provider about introducing new foods to your baby.

Even if you have no reason to be concerned about a food allergy or sensitivity, consider taking a week to introduce each new food. If there are no concerns by the end of the week then start with the next one.

Weekly introduction of new foods:

Day one – introduce a bite or two of the new food at either breakfast or lunch meal only

Day two – feed as much of the new food as they want at either breakfast or lunch only (so, at one meal only)

Day three – feed as much of the new food as they want at two meals

Days four to seven – feed your baby as much of the new food as they want at two or three meals.

As mentioned above, if there is a reaction to a new food, try to wait two months until trying that food again and do not introduce anything new until the symptoms clear up.

Hypoallergenic food introduction chart

6 months
Veggies: carrot, broccoli, asparagus, squash, zucchini, sweet potato, turnip, parsnip, greens, beets
Fruit: prunes
Protein: breastmilk Grains: n/a

7+ months (or 9 months if higher risk)
Veggies: Brussels sprouts, cucumber, celery, peppers, onions, cauliflower
Fruit: banana, avocado, kiwi, cherry, blueberry, blackberry, raspberry, grape, apple
Protein: breastmilk, turkey, chicken, fish, pork, small amount of peanut butter (<2g/week)[6]
Grains: rice, millet, quinoa, amaranth, buckwheat, oats

9 to 12 months
Veggies: cabbage, potato, tomato, green, beans
Fruit: citrus, strawberry, pineapple
Protein: breastmilk, goat milk, beef, lamb
Grains: barley, kamut, spelt, rye

One year (or age 2 if higher risk)
Protein: eggs, shellfish
Grains: wheat, corn

Higher risk foods

As noted in the chart, consider waiting to introduce high allergen foods and foods that are harder on the system to digest until after your baby is a year old. These foods include: meat, wheat, eggs, dairy, soy, nuts, honey and shellfish.

Even proteins can be introduced before whole grains as stomach acid and enzymes for protein digestion are almost at adult levels by six weeks whereas carb enzymes are not at adult levels until 18 months. As shown in the chart, consider waiting until at least nine months before introducing whole grains.

There are also different approaches to introducing infants and children to tree nuts. There was a study that found when infants were exposed to peanuts between five to nine months they were less likely to have anaphylaxis to them by age five. If your healthcare provider supports the introduction of peanuts at this age, it is always best to use natural organic peanut butter and non-hydrogenated, high sugar forms.

Dealing with picky eaters

If your baby doesn't want to eat something, don't make them (remember when your parents used to make you eat your peas and you absolutely can't stand the taste of them to this very day? Eww!).

Instead, try waiting a few weeks or a month then gently introduce it again, they may come around. Don't give up! Some babies take many exposures to new foods before really loving them.

We want infants to develop a lifelong love for vegetables early! When introducing solids, consider starting with vegetables and then fruits. Baby teething feeders can be helpful when you are ready to introduce solid fruits and vegetables and they give parents peace of mind because the mesh keeps the whole pieces of food enclosed.

Also visit our site for more on introducing new foods to children, and how to deal with picky eaters.

The importance of iron from six months onward

After six months a baby's iron stores start to become depleted, this is even more so in Mothers who had low iron levels prior to pregnancy to begin with. Including iron rich foods around this age is important to ensure your baby is getting this very important micronutrient.

Refer to the Ask Dr. Pam Q&A's for food sources of iron for your infant.

Must haves for baby's solid foods

Check out our baby essentials list below and on our site for every stage of your baby's development.

You can pick up cotton baby bibs, burpers and facecloths just about anywhere. But when it comes to keeping your baby's clothes clean after you introduce solids, some of the leather bibs on the market are adorable and functional – they fold up easily and are easy to clean.

Ingredients in your baby's food

Consider fresh local, organic fruits, vegetables and whole grains, certified by the Canadian government or the United States Department of Agriculture (USDA).

Also consider local, organic or free range, hormone free and grass finished meats and dairy.

We try to keep an eye out for non-GMO foods as well because we are not sure how safe genetically modified foods are for people long-term. The Non-GMO Project website is a good resource in terms of helping to keep track of foods that are genetically modified (nongmoproject.org).

How to make your own baby food (if you want to)

Preparing your own baby food fresh daily is best but not always possible. Making your own baby food is not a gold standard so do not feel bad if you do not have the time or desire to do it. If you want to make some baby food yourself, consider pureeing your meats and adding them to store bought pureed fruits and vegetables.

Below are the steps for making baby food from a single ingredient but the process is the same for baby food that contains more than one ingredient. For more than one ingredient (including fruits and veggies, grains, cooked meats or fish and sauces), combine the ingredients when cooking or cook separately and combine ingredients when you are pureeing the foods.

To help save time, consider making a week or two worth of baby food at a time because life can get a bit hectic with little ones. You could make as much baby food as you like as long as you can freeze or store it for later use. Baby food can be stored for up to two or three days in the refrigerator. Frozen baby food is typically good for up to one month, or longer if in a deep freeze.

Making baby food isn't difficult but it does take time. If you're up for it, here's how in four easy steps.

Step 1 for making your own baby food: Prep the food.

Thoroughly washing fruits and vegetables and peel the rind or skin if there is any. Cut up fruit or vegetable into smaller pieces for cooking (the smaller you cut it up, the faster it cooks). You do not need to cut up certain foods such as spinach as it easily purees in whole form.

Step 2: Cook or steam your food.

Do not overcook fruits and vegetables to help preserve as much of the vitamins and nutrients possible. Reserve a cup or two of the water your food or vegetable was cooked in and set aside.

Step 3: Puree your baby food.

Put your cooked foods into your blender, food processor or baby food maker device. When pureeing fruits and vegetables, add a bit of the reserved water you set aside and puree, adding more water (if needed) depending on the consistency you would like your baby food. You can add less water when you're pureeing as your baby gets older to introduce more texture to your baby's food.

Step 4: Store your baby food.

Pour your pureed food into ice cube trays with lids (to freeze and store for later use) or into pouches or mini mason jars (to store in the refrigerator). To help save space in your freezer, put the frozen cubes into freezer bags – you could put a number of different flavours of frozen cubes into each freezer bag so that when you thaw each bag your baby will have a variety of foods to choose from! Don't forget to date and label your trays, jars or other baby food packages.

It is much more convenient to use a high quality baby food blender and to freeze the food in batches. Check our site for more tips on making baby food, including storage containers we recommend.

Healthy sleep practices

Reducing the risk of sudden infant death syndrome (SIDS)

Healthcare providers generally recommend a number of things to help avoid suffocation and reduce the risk of SIDS. Recommendations commonly include ensuring absolutely nothing is in a baby's crib (or bassinet) with them when going to sleep. This means no stuffed animals, pillows, blankets, bumper pads, bottles, etc., and making sure these things and any cords (for baby monitors, etc.) are outside of your baby's reach.

Keep babies completely clear of any trace of cigarette smoke. Do not let your baby sit or sleep in a bucket car seat for longer than 1.5 hours at a time.

Putting a baby on their back to sleep could also reduce the risk of SIDS. Adult supervised tummy time during awake or play time is okay but never put your baby down on their stomach to sleep.

There are mixed views on whether or not you should co-sleep with your baby. One solution if you'd like your baby to sleep close to you, but not in bed with you, is to put them in a bassinet right beside your bed.

Consult with your healthcare provider about reducing the risk of SIDS.

Investing in a baby monitor with a video camera

Since babies are able to sense when someone is in the room, it can be difficult to check on them inconspicuously and without waking them. Video camera monitors allow you to check on your baby quickly and conveniently.

Always go to check on your baby in person if you are concerned for their health or wellbeing.

How long to let your baby cry for

This is a controversial topic and really up to you based on your healthcare provider's recommendations. If you've implemented all of the healthy practices in this program, it is less likely you will need to let your baby to cry much at all. That's an important aspect of this program.

The older they are the louder and longer they cry. This program is meant to help avoid baby and toddler sleep training and all the tears that come along with it!

We typically don't like to let babies cry longer than 15 minutes at a time if you are teaching them to self soothe as a newborn. Consider starting with five and then 10 minute intervals of tears maximum. There are a lot more information and tips for soothing below.

Teaching baby to be patient

If you use this program, do not be surprised if your baby eventually starts to wake up from a nap or in the morning, cooing or laying silently in their crib looking around. If your baby wakes up in the middle of a sleep or if they are upset waking from sleep time, check their monitor or go to them immediately if you are concerned for their wellbeing.

If you are not concerned for your baby's wellbeing, we recommend waiting about five minutes or so before going to pick them up after they wake up. This can also be an important first step if your baby is used to falling asleep on you at nap or bedtime. Your baby will learn to wake by themselves and know that you are going to come and get them.

Swaddling until ready to transition to a sleep sack

Consider swaddling your baby at nap time at least for the first few weeks following birth your baby. Swaddling creates a sense of warmth, snugness and comfort for babies, like being inside of the womb. It can also help prevent a baby from being impacted by their startle reflex to help with longer, uninterrupted sleep.

Swaddling is most effective when a square blanket is used. Traditionally babies arms are wrapped snugly (straight at the side) in a swaddle, with the hips and legs more loose. However, it is important to ask your healthcare provider exactly how they recommend you swaddle because some now suggest leaving one arm out of the swaddle for safety reasons. Always make sure that the swaddle does not unravel or cover their head. Stop swaddling if your baby can get out of their swaddle.

Babies typically transition from a swaddle to sleep sack between three to six months but the timing will depend on you and your baby. When you decide your baby is ready to make the transition, start by leaving one arm out of the sleep sack for a few weeks (if you're not already leaving one arm loose on your healthcare providers' recommendations). Stop swaddling if your baby can get out of their swaddle, or if your baby begins to start rolling over from their back to stomach while sleeping.

When your baby is ready, consider transitioning from a swaddle to a sleep sack. There are a variety of swaddle styles that allow for easy access to change diapers. See our site for our favorites.

Putting baby to sleep in their crib while awake

It is completely normal for your baby to fall asleep on you each time, at least for the first few weeks. And it's such a lovely bonding experience.

But newborn babies can sleep 14 or more hours in a 24 hour period. As your baby gets older, consider if you would like them to be able to fall asleep on their own in their own crib rather than being dependent on the comfort of you or an adult to fall asleep. Consider mixing it up from nap to nap so that baby will be able to fall asleep both ways.

One thing that can help babies get comfortable going to sleep in their own crib for naps and at bedtime by themselves is if they are awake when you put them down from day one. This may be difficult to do for the first few weeks because newborns tend to sleep so much, but the sooner you are able to start doing this the easier it will be.

Communicate what time it is and create a bit of a pattern by giving your baby a hug and letting them know that it is nap or bedtime each time you are putting them down to sleep. Even if your baby is asleep on you or groggy when you put them down (more likely as a newborn because they are less alert than older babies). If you tell them what time it is, they will get used to hearing it and know you will come back and pick them up again when they wake up.

Avoiding dependence on sleep props

Props include things like sleep swings, rocking chairs, ambient or nature sounds, mobiles, soothers. As your baby gets older, sleep props may include things like stuffed animals.

Whether or not you use props regularly to calm or put your baby to sleep is going to depend on your preferences. Worst case is that you could risk always needing a prop with you to help your baby (or toddler or preschooler) fall asleep – and heaven forbid you forget it, or lose it, risking a complete meltdown!

Consider using props in moderation. For example, only give your baby a soother only when out in public, when they are in their car seat, or if they are crying. Keep an extra soother handy when going out in public, and especially when travelling (don't forget your pacifier clip so that you don't drop your soother). Teething jewellery can also come in handy while on the go.

Teaching baby to fall asleep in any environment

This can be helpful if you'd like your baby to be able to sleep anytime and anywhere, whether you are out for a few hours doing errands or if you plan to take a family vacation. Like adults, not all babies will sleep as soundly as others. A few helpful suggestions are below.

First, switch up the crib and room that your baby sleeps in regularly to help ensure that they do not get accustomed to sleeping only in one place. This can be done more easily if you have a portable crib, bassinet, playpen or travel crib.

Put your baby down to sleep in the same room as an older sibling periodically from when they are a newborn onward (in their own crib) so that your children can get used to sleeping in the same room. This will help to ensure flexibility when travelling since your kids may need to sleep in the same room when you are on a family vacation.

Also consider switching up the level and type of background noise when you put your baby down for naps and bedtime. This includes putting your baby's crib in quiet rooms as well as rooms where people are talking or kids are playing, where music is playing or television is on, and where someone is vacuuming in the background.

If your baby will be in a home with animals, consider keeping the door to the room shut or using a travel crib with a cover to help prevent pets from trying to sleep with them (especially cats because they have been known to like to snuggle up with or on).

Ensure that your child is able to sleep in their car seat as well as sitting up or laying down in a stroller, so that your baby can nap on the go. It can also be helpful if your baby will fall asleep on you in a baby carrier. Depending on your schedule, if your baby starts to fall asleep in their car seat, stroller or in their baby carrier on a regular basis when it is not nap time, you may want to wake them up. For safety reasons, do not let your baby sleep in a bucket car seat for longer than 1.5 hours.

Avoiding an overtired baby

Babies that are well-rested tend to go to sleep quicker and with less fuss simply because they are not overtired. Well-rested babies also have a tendency to sleep longer at night as compared to when they are overtired. Common ways babies can get overtired is if you regularly skip naps or keep them awake longer during the day before bedtime.

Eliminating daily naps too early can also cause them to get overtired. Consider teaching your baby how to nap even if you don't think that they want to. An adequate amount of sleep is important to your baby's growth and development, something to ask your healthcare provider about. Dropping a nap too early can cause a less than ideal chain reaction – your baby will likely be overtired and cranky if they don't nap, which usually means that it will be harder to put them down at night.

Some parents find that the earlier they put their baby down at bedtime the longer they will sleep at night if their tummy is full. For example, if you if you put your baby down at 8:00 p.m. they may only sleep nine or 10 hours but if it's closer to 7:00 p.m., they will sleep 10 to 12 hours.

The value of quiet time

Your child may need a half hour to three hour nap each day (or every few days, and eventually on weekends only) at least until they are school age. However, your child may drop all of their naps or be ready to reduce the length of their naps early as early as 12 to 18 months which we discuss below. There is so much life-long value in gently teaching your baby and child how to just *be* with themselves, quietly playing, laying and sitting quietly on their own.

Once your child starts to drop their naps, consider introducing the concept of quiet time for 30 minutes to an hour, or even up to 1.5 hours each day. This can be helpful for you and your child after lunch where they can play alone in their crib or playpen. If your child is not ready to go to sleep at night they can lay quietly in their bed as well.

Helpful homeopathic remedies for sleep, etc.

If your baby has a cold, we have found that Boiron Laboratories' Coryzalia homeopathic medicine for babies is very effective, as is their homeopathic Camilia for teething, restlessness and irritability. Boiron Laboratories also has a homeopathic remedy for flu-like symptoms called Oscillococcinum. There are also homeopathic remedies for restlessness and disorders associated with restlessness such as irritability and mild sleeping disorders (occasional sleeplessness, nightmares and night terrors) called Quietude, and Windi homeopathic Gas and Colic Relief. Your Naturopath can recommend and many health stores these homeopathics (also find out more on our site).

We have suggestions to help with teething on our site, including using an amber necklace. Most baby stores carry amber necklaces for babies however sometimes babies become aware of and pull on them, especially if you do not put it on them from day one to get used to.

We have found that placenta tincture can be an effective way to help to calm babies. It can also be helpful for Mom's, as are placenta capsules. We sincerely believe that these are more precious than gold and encourage you to keep an open mind about the potential benefits before you decide.

Read more about this on our site and ask your Naturopath for a referral to a person or company that provides placenta encapsulation services near you. If you are in Canada, the U.S. or Mexico, check out www.purebirth.ca. If you don't have a Naturopath, you can contact us as we may be able to recommend someone who provides these services near you.

Tips when travelling with baby

The flexibility of the schedule below helps allow parents to more easily switch to a new time zone within four hours of their normal time zone within a day or two upon arrival without much trouble.

A few things to consider. Since each baby is different, pick and choose what to do depending on what works better for you and your family.

First, you may find it helpful to adjust your baby's feeding schedule forward or back half an hour each day for the week or so before you depart on your trip to help get ahead of the time change.

It can also help a lot if you can keep your baby awake for as long as possible until you arrive at your destination. Preferably, keep them up until you arrive at the new destination, or only let them have a short nap on the plane. Then when you arrive, feed your baby, put them down, and then wake them up based on the new time zone. If the time change is more than four hours you will need to adjust this approach.

There are a few other things worth mentioning when travelling with a baby. First, always have extra liquids and solids, diapers and clothes with you in your carry-on when you travel just in case it takes longer than you think to arrive at your destination. Also keep a few soothers handy – letting your baby breastfeed or drink their bottle, or suck on a soother during take off and landing of an airplane can be very helpful for popping their ears.

If you find your baby is anxious or crying when travelling, consider trying Boiron Laboratories' Camilia. Bringing your own car seat and travel crib may be a bit annoying, but may be worth it if it gives you peace of mind in terms of safety.

Check out our site for our top tips on on travelling with babies and children stress-free.

Tips specific to your baby's schedule

The tips below can be helpful no matter what schedule you are using with your baby.

Feeding every three hours with a nap in between

We typically recommend naps between 1.5 to three hours in length to help create a consistent schedule and facilitate dropping the nighttime feedings more smoothly.

Never wake a sleeping baby, right? Not necessarily!

Even if your baby is able to sleep longer than the recommended periods in each stage, think twice before letting them continue to sleep longer. This can be so difficult at first when you are already sleep deprived (we get it and have been there!). However, we think that the work up front with our schedule is well worth it so that your baby can sleep through the night uninterrupted at 12 weeks.

Waking between feedings or at night

There will be times when your baby wakes up unexpectedly in the middle of a nap or at night because of a wet or dirty diaper,
nightmare or night terror, cold or flu, or teething. If your baby wakes up hungry, it may be because they did not have enough liquids or solids during the day, or they may be going through a growth spurt.

If your baby is hungry when they wake up, feed them. If baby is 12 months or older, a different snack may be appropriate, such as milk of choice in a sippy cup. If you find that your baby is making a habit out of waking up in the middle of the night for a feeding (regardless of whether it is a whole feeding or just a small snack), make sure they are getting enough during the day. A bottle may be helpful if you're finding that baby wakes for your breast as a comfort rather than due to hunger.

Stirring in the morning

Your baby may stir or even wake up (and coo or talk or cry) in the early morning hours between 4:00 a.m. or 5:00 a.m., then fall back asleep. If you can, give them five to 15 minutes to chill out and self sooth. Babies will often fall back asleep within a few minutes if you leave them alone this early in the morning.

Unless you are concerned for your baby's health and wellbeing, always consider waiting a few minutes before you go and pick your baby up to teach patience and make sure they are actually ready to get up.

Getting off track and then back on again

It's okay if you get off track! It is completely normal for your baby to get off track for a day or two, or even a few hours each day for a few weeks, especially if you are on vacation. The whole point of this program is to create a consistent schedule up front to allow for a lot of flexibility!

Getting back on track isn't too difficult, especially if you've been somewhat consistent with your baby's schedule. Most of the time you should be able to get your baby back on track by letting them sleep for a slightly shorter or longer period of time between feedings later that day or at night. It depends on when you get off track of course.

If you need to feed your baby in between feedings, regardless of whether it is during a nap or in the middle of the night, try to wake them up within an hour of the next scheduled feeding time for a whole feeding as usual. Often times your baby just needs an extra feeding, particularly if they are going through a growth spurt. Although your baby may eat less at the next feeding, they will likely have normal feedings after that.

Until you know your baby has a full tummy in less time, feed for up to 1.5 hours. Your baby should eventually have a full feeding within an hour and then half an hour. This can happen sooner than you may think.

Know how to soothe your baby

Self soothing at sleep time (newborns crying it out)

At some point you will need to let your baby cry it out to sleep. With this schedule it tends to be one to 30 minutes when your baby is a newborn. To us, the fewer the tears the better, especially over the long run.

Unfortunately, the same tricks will not always work for every baby so there is a bit of trial and error until you get to know your baby. Ideally, within a matter of weeks, your baby will simply fall asleep when you put them down because they know what is going on and they are comfortable with your well established schedule.

Although this feeding and sleep program involves an element of teaching your baby to self soothe, we absolutely do not promote your baby crying to sleep. Ideally, you've done all the checks and baby so you know they're comfortable, and then they simply close their eyes and go to sleep on their own once you put them in their crib. Or perhaps your baby fusses for up to about five minutes or so before falling asleep on their own. But this is not always the case, especially if you have not been doing this from day one!

It is not easy to hear your baby cry, period. And although we believe teaching your baby to self soothe is an important skill that can be helpful for the rest of your child's life, we do not recommend letting your newborn cry for longer than 15 minutes without picking them up giving them a hug and letting them know that it is ok. Always check on your baby if you are concerned for their health or wellbeing

As we mentioned above, depending on how old your baby is, you would go in and check on them between a few up to 30 minutes. In the first two weeks, we do not promote letting your baby crying longer than a minute or two. From there, three, five or up to 10 minutes if your baby is a newborn.

Sleep training

For others, teaching your baby about bedtime can involve sleep training and take all night and more than one night. Sleep training can be very hard on parents and their children, especially if your baby is six months or older, and if you need to break well established sleep habits.

The self soothing process

It can be easier to start this when your baby is more tired like at a nighttime feeding rather than when they are more alert during the day at nap time, especially of your baby is used to falling asleep on you before you put them down.

Depending on what you are comfortable with and how old your baby is, you may decide not to go into your crying baby's room at all if you are sleep training or if you are teaching them to self sooth.

If you do go into your baby's room when they are crying (which we recommend when your baby is a newborn), you may want to take the opportunity to check to make sure they have not vomited in their crib. Also check if they are comfortable in terms of temperature and clothing, and that they don't need a diaper change, etc. Then, start by putting your hand on your baby's chest, gently rubbing, while firmly letting them know it's okay and that it's bedtime (and time to close their eyes and go to sleep), before walking out of their room. If you pick them up for a hug, be firm on the fact that it is sleep time and promptly put them back down again. Repeat this as many times as needed.

Depending on your baby's personality and when they are finding their voice, a random cry here and there is completely normal. As they get older, your baby may even go through a stage where they cry just because they realize they can (or fake cries for attention – you will recognize it when it happens). However, if they are still crying after 30 minutes something may be wrong.

This is where the Dunstan Baby Language and having a camera baby monitor can be very helpful.

Top tips for soothing a crying baby

Sorry to say, but there will likely be a time (or many) when you need to soothe your crying baby. Over time you will figure out what works best for your baby. As a starting point, consider trying these "calming womb-like sensations" which have been coined "the 5 S's" by Dr.Harvey Karp.[7]

Here are a few of our thoughts on the 5 S's.

The first S is to swaddle your baby before putting them down to sleep.

We've already discussed above and completely agree especially with a newborn. Note that eventually your baby will grow out of swaddling.

The second S it to calm your baby by using the side or stomach position.

This means that you hold them in one of three ways. Either on their side, on their stomach or over your shoulder. When your baby is calm, place them on their back to sleep for safety reasons.

The third S is to make use of a "shush" sound.

While in the womb, babies hear a fair amount of blood flowing through their Mother's blood vessels and movement of her stomach and intestines. You just mimick this noise to calm your baby. There are many white noise machines on the market (the Happiest Baby's six specially engineered sounds to calm crying and boost sleep). Depending on your preferences in terms of habits and sleep props, you may not want your baby to become reliant on white noise to fall asleep. Just something to think about.

The fourth S is use of the swing.

This simulates the jiggly sensation a baby feels in their Mother's womb. It has been described by Dr. Karp as follows: "Imagine your baby bopping around inside your belly when you jaunt down the stairs! While slow rocking is fine for keeping quiet babies calm, you need to use fast, tiny motions to soothe a crying infant mid-squawk. To do it, always support the head/neck, keep your motions small; and move no more than 1 inch back and forth." *If you try this remember not to ever shake your baby!*

As you may know, there are a number of baby swings on the market as well as rocking chairs. But again, depending on your preferences in terms of habits and sleep props, you may not want your baby to become reliant on these props to fall asleep.

The fifth S is to give your baby something to suck on.

We discussed this above, and should note that a soother can be very helpful when you are teaching your baby to self soothe to sleep. Unless you know your baby will not take a pacifier, it's not a bad idea to always have one on hand in case you need it. The need to suck is an innate way for a baby to feel calm and relaxed. Some babies even suck their thumbs in the womb!

If you are unable to calm your baby, consult with your healthcare provider to rule out colic or illness.

Colic and health concerns

It can be very challenging if your baby is colicky or if there are any health concerns. There are no rules! This is where your chart is important in terms of tracking when your baby is crying in a day, and making observations about your baby in the *comments* section. It will be easy to convey this information to your baby's healthcare provider if and when required.

The key is to get to the underlying cause of why your baby is upset. As mentioned above, it is important to do all the check to make sure baby is comfortable, but there could be underlying issues.

For example, if you are having nursing difficulties, they can be the result of tensions and restrictions in a baby's head, spine or body. Restrictions can be caused by pressures experienced during late pregancy, and childbirth, especially if the pressure of birth is increased by fast, long or induced labours, caesarean births, or forceps or vacuum assisted vaginal deliveries. It's not a bad idea to consult with your baby's healthcare provider about using craniosacral therapy to treat these types of concerns with your newborn or infant. Physiotherapy and osteopath treatments can also be very helpful for babies, including helping to assist with latching issues.

All things to consult with your baby's healthcare provider about.

Baby feeding and sleep schedule

Many parents have used this program as a starting point and have adapted it to meet the unique needs of their family. You can use it prescriptively or as a general reference guide. Do what works best for you and your family!

The purpose of the tested schedule below is to help you gently transition your baby to a flexible schedule that works for your family (and an uninterrupted night of sleep between 10 to 12 weeks).

Phases (or stages) for sleeping through the night & your baby's chart

We have broken the schedule down into phases (or stages) with the intention that at each one your baby begins to sleep longer through the night. You can put these on your fridge or other convenient place beside your baby's chart for ease of reference.

Regardless of whether you are starting this schedule in weeks one or two after birth, or if are starting later, the starting point is to focus on tracking your baby's feeding and sleep cycles on their chart. From there, you will slowly transition to feed once every three hours. We get into more about this transition below.

Sample baby charts

The sample charts that accompany this program are intentionally hand-written, and don't look pretty and organized. This is because they are real. These charts were literally pulled and copied directly from the charts of the babies of co-creator Tereza Fonda. Parenting is often tiring, messy and disorganized!

We're committed to help make it all easier for you!

6:00 or 7:00 a.m. breakfast time feeding

The sample charts that accompany this program were prepared based on a 6:00 a.m. breakfast time. This breakfast time is conducive to a feeding between 5:00 a.m. and 7:00 a.m. once your schedule is established. This timing is great for Mothers and parents who want to have breakfast with their children before they have to be somewhere in the morning and/or need time to drop their kids off or arrange childcare first. Then, feed lunch at noon-ish and dinner around 6:00 p.m.

If you can't decide on a suitable breakfast time, keep in mind that a 7:00 a.m. breakfast time would be conducive to a feeding window between 6:00 a.m. and 8:00 a.m. once your schedule is established. The initial lunch and dinner times would be at 1:00 p.m. and 7:00 p.m. However, you would be able to tweak the schedule over time to feed your baby earlier or later after you have established your schedule.

We don't recommend selecting a breakfast time any later unless you would like to consistently feed lunch at or after 2:00 p.m. and dinner at or after 8:00 p.m. Plus, you can go back to sleep right after the breakfast feeding if you're using this schedule anyway.

We recognize that 6:00 a.m. and 7:00 a.m. feeding times may sound really early, especially if you have had grown accustomed to the luxury of sleeping for 10 plus hours each night and laying in bed until noon (at least on weekends). No worries, we have a solution for this.

The solution is that you have the option of putting your baby down for their early morning nap promptly after you feed them breakfast and going back to sleep until their snack time at 9:00 a.m. – for best results, train your baby to go down for their nap about five to ten minutes after finishing their breakfast feeding as soon as you start this program. You should be able to successfully do this until around six months, at which time your baby may want to be awake for longer periods of time after breakfast. This is a great option for any parent who would appreciate extra sleep during the day.

Phase 1: Weeks 1 and 2 – surviving the first two weeks

This tends to be the most challenging stage by far especially for Mothers who are caring for their new baby, healing from childbirth, and sleep deprived. But we believe the work up front is worth it, especially if you value sleep for yourself and your family! Consistent feeding times and full tummies are key to helping transition baby to your schedule with as little fuss possible.

At this stage baby may fall asleep on you during feedings before they are full, which is why we recommend a 1.5 hour *feeding window* – try to top baby up within the last 15 minutes of each feeding window unless you already know they have a full tummy. There may only be an hour to rest from the end of one feeding to the start of the next. Be patient... babies get older they usually feed much faster.

A few important notes for this stage are that we recommend 5-15 minute cuddles before putting baby down is awake or play time at this stage. You could put baby down for tummy time too, etc. Refer to the sample baby charts for each phase below.

Phase 1 suggested schedule

6:00 a.m. – first feeding of the day (breakfast time)
- Baby may already be awake – wake baby up between 5:30 and 6:30 a.m. (ideally, no earlier than 5:00 a.m., no later than 7:00 a.m.)
- Feed for up to 1.5 hours from the time you start (this will be shorter than 1.5 hour if you know baby is full sooner)
- Cuddle, burp, diaper change, etc., for 5-15 minutes
- Put baby down for nap time (1.5 to 3 hours)

9:00 a.m. – next feeding time (morning snack time)
- Wake up baby & start feeding between 8:30 a.m. and 9:30 a.m. (no earlier than 8:00 a.m., no later than 10:00 a.m.)
- Feed for up to 1.5 hours from the time you start
- Cuddle, burp, diaper change, etc., for 5-15 minutes
- Put baby down for nap time (1.5 to 3 hours)

12:00 p.m. – next feeding time (lunch time)
- Wake up baby & start feeding between 11:30 a.m. and 12:30 p.m. (no earlier than 11:00 a.m., no later than 1:00 p.m.)
- Feed for up to 1.5 hours from the time you start
- Cuddle, burp, diaper change, etc., for 5-15 minutes
- Put baby down for nap time (1.5 to 3 hours)

3:00 p.m. – next feeding time (afternoon snack time)
- Wake up baby & start feeding between 2:30 p.m. and 3:30 p.m.
  (no earlier than 2:00 p.m., no later than 4:00 p.m.)
- Feed for up to 1.5 hours from the time you start
- Cuddle, burp, diaper change, etc., for 5-15 minutes
- Put baby down for nap time (1.5 to 3 hours)

6:00 p.m. – next feeding time (dinner time and bedtime top up)
- Wake up baby & start feeding between 5:30 p.m. and 6:30 p.m.
  (no earlier than 5:00 p.m., no later than 7:00 p.m.)
- Feed for up to one hour from the time you start
- Bedtime routine (e.g. brush gums, sponge bath/wash face, story, etc.)
- Top baby up 15 minutes before bedtime
- Cuddle, burp, diaper change, and put baby down for bedtime (1.5 to 3 hours)

9:00 p.m. – night feeding time (temporary feed, leave sleepsack/swaddle on)
- Wake up baby & start feeding between 8:30 p.m. and 9:30 p.m.
  (no earlier than 8:00 p.m., no later than 10:00 p.m.)
- Feed for up to 1.5 hours from the time you start
  (in a dimly lit, quiet room – whisper, minimize talking)
- Burp, diaper change, hug, etc.
- Put baby back down for bedtime (1.5 to 3 hours)

12:00 a.m. – night feeding time (temporary, leave sleepsack/swaddle on)
- Wake up baby & start feeding between 11:30 p.m. and 12:30 a.m.
  (no earlier than 11:00 p.m., no later than 1:00 a.m.)
- Feed for up to 1.5 hours from the time you start
  (in a dimly lit, quiet room – whisper, minimize talking)
- Burp, diaper change, hug, etc.
- Put baby back down for bedtime (1.5 to 3 hours)

3:00 a.m. – night feeding time (temporary, leave sleepsack/swaddle on)
- Wake up baby & start feeding between 2:30 a.m. and 3:30 a.m.
  (no earlier than 2:00 a.m., no later than 4:00 a.m.)
- Feed for up to 1.5 hours from the time you start
- (in a dimly lit, quiet room – whisper, minimize talking)
- Burp, diaper change, hug, etc.
- Put baby back down for bedtime (1.5 to 3 hours)

Feeding once every three hours (8 times in 24 hours)

There are a number of reasons why your baby may need to feed more often than once every three hours, especially as a newborn. This could be due to health concerns like blood glucose issues, dehydration, jaundice, or to make sure baby is gaining enough weight. Other reasons could be that your baby is not getting enough milk (not latching properly if breastfeeding) or that your baby is going through a growth spurt and wakes up for a whole feeding an hour and a half after they've just had a whole feeding. Feeding more frequently could also be a habit or a personal preference which is okay as long as it works for you!

We believe the sooner you are able to feed your baby once every three hours the better because it will allow for more predictability and rest for new parents. Our tips to help with the transition to feeding once every three hours are below.

First, be intentional about when you start the transition to feeding every three hours. Start the transition at a feeding when you think your baby will drink a fair amount to fill their tummy before going down for 1.5 to 2.5 hour nap afterward.

This is especially important if you find that they eat more at some feedings than others. You may find that your baby tends to drink more at the 6:00 a.m. breakfast, noon lunch and 6:00 p.m. dinner/bedtime top up feedings and slightly less in between feedings. You may find this especially when they are 12 weeks old and sleeping 10 to 12 hours uninterrupted at night.

Consider waiting until baby has just had a small prior feeding, or baby is waking from a long nap and hasn't been feeding for at least two hours. Try to start as close as possible to one of the feeding times you circled on baby's feeding chart (i.e. within half an hour of that specific feeding time). So you will probably be feeding every three hours starting at either 6:00 a.m. or 7:00 a.m. for breakfast. If possible, consider starting the transition at breakfast one morning.

Second, keep track on your baby's chart of when baby is feeding and how much they're having each time. Also keep track of the things that can cause you to get off track of your preferred schedule, like teething, growth spurts and colds and flu's. Habits can also cause you to get off track such as ongoing missed naps or late bedtime. This was everything is easier for you to reference.

Third, focus on 1.5 hour feeding windows (or less if you know your baby's tummy is full before that time). We talk about this a lot.

Tips for Phase 1 weeks 1 and 2 (try not to let baby cry, hold them!)

Feeding tips for weeks 1 and 2

- Baby will be drinking breastmilk or formula only until around 6 months.

- Baby may already be awake at feeding time. If it's too early but they are hungry, feed and adjust their schedule accordingly throughout the day.

- During the day, unswaddle baby or take sleepsack off for *awake* time.

- Tell baby what time it is (breakfast, lunch, dinner, bed, play, etc.).

- Despite suggested feeding start times, try to be as consistent as possible at this point. Ideally, start each feeding every 3 hours from the time you started the last one (circled on your baby's chart).

- If baby isn't ready to eat at feeding time, or falls asleep/needs a break during a feeding, let them rest for up to half an hour (let play, snuggle or sleep on you) – repeat as needed.

- Make sure baby's full before nap/bed time. To ensure baby gets a whole feeding, you may end up feeding them off and on for 1.5 hours, and then topping them up during the last 15 minutes before their sleep time.

- If baby falls asleep on you toward the end of the 1.5 hour feeding window after they are full, don't worry too much about waking them up before you put them down for a sleep at this point.

Sleep tips for weeks 1 and 2

- Wait at least 5 minutes after feeding before putting down, swaddled or in their sleepsack. Baby is likely to fall asleep on you while feeding at this stage so this will likely be cuddle time!

- If possible, before you put baby down to sleep, try to gently wake baby at least so they can hear you whisper to go to sleep for nap or bedtime.

- Eventually you will want baby to be awake when you put them down. But for now, even if they are asleep get in the habit of saying it's nap/bedtime.

- At night feedings, consider feeding in a dimly lit, quiet room and whispering to help teach baby it's night time.

- At night feedings, leave sleepsack on and no play time – snuggles only!

- Before you put baby down for a nap or bedtime, always make sure they have a fully tummy, are well burped and are comfy (clean diaper, etc.).

- Each sleep time (day or night) should be 1.5 to 3 hours long (1.5 to 2 hours is optimal). Lay baby down to sleep for the majority of that time.

Phase 2: Weeks 3 to 7 – establishing your schedule

This phase is generally the same as the prior stage except that you have the option of dropping the 3:00 a.m. feeding (or midnight feeding if preferred), so that baby sleeps up to six hours.* Do not drop any feeding until you are sure baby is ready – make sure baby has had a consistent routine in the prior stage for at least a week or two.

Phase 2 suggested schedule

6:00 a.m. – breakfast time feeding, same as above

9:00 a.m. – morning feeding time, same as above

12:00 p.m. – lunch time feeding, same as above

3:00 p.m. – afternoon feeding time, same as above

6:00 p.m. – dinner feed time (and bedtime top up), same as above

9:00 p.m. – night feed (temporary, sleepsack/swaddle on), same as above

12:00 a.m. – night feed (temporary, sleepsack/swaddle on), same as above

3:00 a.m. – optional night feed (temporary, leave sleepsack/swaddle on)*

*The 3:00 a.m. feeding with be the same as above until you are ready to drop this feeding. We do not recommend dropping this 3:00 a.m. feeding (or midnight feeding if preferred) until your baby's feeding and sleep schedule has been consistent for at least a week. Note: Refer to the tips and the sample baby charts for each phase below.

Dropping the midnight feeding at this stage and then the 3:00 a.m. feeding at the next stage can work too. We haven't had as many parents go this route but dropping the midnight feeding first may work better if you started the schedule with an older baby, or if you find that baby is super sleepy at the midnight feeding (i.e., if it just feels right for your family at this stage to feed around 9:00 p.m., then again around 3:00 a.m., and then at the 6:00 a.m. breakfast feeding).

As baby gets older, they will become more alert and be able to stay awake for longer. During the day, let them play before feeding (if it's too early to feed or if baby is not ready to eat), and afterward even if it's only for five minutes, to help establish *feeding times* or *windows*. Once your schedule is established, baby may know what time it is, being hungry at feeding time and sleepy at nap/bedtime.

Tips for Phase 2 weeks 3 to 7 (gentle, patient but persistent & consistent)

Feeding tips for weeks 3 to 7

- Refer to the above tips for weeks 1 and 2 as they still apply.
- You may still end up feeding baby on and off for 1.5 hours to ensure they get a whole feeding – try to top them up during the last 15 minutes before sleep time. If baby needs a break or falls asleep during a feeding, wait for up to half an hour then try again – repeat as needed.
- Hopefully baby will be awake when you put them down. Try to be more aware of this during this phase to help them learn it is okay to fall asleep on their own rather than in your arms each time.
- If baby is full and falls asleep on you toward the end of the 1.5 hour feeding window, don't go out of your way to wake them up before you put them down for a sleep. If they're asleep and you don't think they have a full tummy yet, consider topping them up quickly before you put them down for their nap or bedtime.
- We wouldn't let a baby cry for more than 5 to 10 minutes at this stage (everything is still so new and they need your comfort).

Sleep tips for weeks 3 to 7 (dropping the 3:00 a.m. (midnight feeding if preferred))

- Refer to the above tips for weeks 1 and 2 as they still apply.
- Baby may stir or wake temporarily when you first drop a feeding so, unless you are concerned for their wellbeing, give them 5-15 minutes to make sure they're actually hungry before going to get them.
- If this 3:00 a.m. feeding is dropped but you find baby is waking up an hour early hungry for breakfast, try to push the 9:00 p.m. and 12:00 a.m. feedings back half an hour to 9:30 p.m. and 12:30 a.m.
- If this 3:00 a.m. feeding is dropped and baby is waking earlier than 5:00 a.m. hungry, treat the feeding like it is a night feeding and push back breakfast to 6:30 a.m. or 7:00 a.m. Then adjust baby's schedule slightly for the rest of the day until you are back on track which should be possible to do by mid or end of the day.
- Watch for habits. If baby is waking before 5:00 a.m. regularly, they may not be ready so go back to stage one and continue feeding at 3:00 a.m. until baby is ready. Try to be as consistent as possible.

Phase 3: Weeks 8 to 11 – maintain routine & drop feedings

This phase is generally the same as the prior stage but you now have the option to drop the midnight feeding (Or 3:00 a.m. feeding if the midnight feeding has already been dropped) so baby sleeps up to eight hours.* Do not drop feedings until baby is ready – make sure baby has had a consistent routine for at least a week or two.

Phase 3 suggested schedule

6:00 a.m. – **breakfast time feeding, same as above**

9:00 a.m. – **morning feeding time, same as above**

12:00 p.m. – **lunch time feeding, same as above**

3:00 p.m. – **afternoon feeding time, same as above**

6:00 p.m. – **dinner time feeding (bedtime top up), same as above**

9:00 p.m. – **night feed (temporary, sleepsack/swaddle on), same as above**

12:00 a.m. – **optional night feeding (temporary, sleepsack/swaddle on)***

*The 12:00 a.m. feeding will be the same as above until you are ready to drop this feeding. We do not recommend dropping this feeding unless baby's schedule has been consistent for a few weeks since dropping the 3:00 a.m. feeding. Refer to tips below.

Note: Refer to the sample baby charts for each phase below.

Tips for Phase 3 weeks 8 to 11 (gentle, patient, persistent & consistent)

Feeding tips for weeks 8 to 11

- Refer to the above tips as they still apply.

- As time goes on, baby will become more alert and be able to stay awake for longer periods of time. Establish clear feeding windows.

- During day, if baby is awake and it's too early to feed (if they are not ready yet), let them play first. Always let them play afterward, even if only for 5 minutes. Like clockwork, baby may know what time it is.

- Although baby may be feeding more quickly at this point, you may still end up feeding on and off for 1.5 hours sometimes to ensure they get a whole feeding. It's still okay to try to top baby up during the last 15 minutes of the 1.5 hour feeding window, before sleep time.

- Baby shouldn't really be falling asleep regularly during feedings at this point. If they need a break during a feeding, wait for up to half an hour then try again – repeat as needed.

- If baby falls asleep on you toward the end of the 1.5 hour feeding window after they're full, gently wake up before putting down to sleep.

- We don't recommend letting baby cry for more than 10 minutes at a time at this age to self-soothe (we just don't have the heart).

Sleep tips for weeks 8 to 11
(dropping the 12:00 a.m. feeding (or 3:00 a.m. if already dropped))

- Refer to the above tips as they still apply.

- Do not drop midnight feeding unless baby's schedule has been consistent for a few weeks since dropping the 3:00 a.m. feeding.

- Ideally, baby is sleeping so well at this point that you either have to wake them for breakfast, or they wake up cooing rather than starving.

- The more you can feed before bedtime the better, especially now that baby is sleeping longer at night.

- When baby has had as much as you think they will eat and drink at dinner and needs a break, continue on with their bedtime routine – they will probably drink a bit extra at the bedtime top up.

- You may find it may makes sense to start feeding baby dinner half an hour earlier to create a bigger spread between dinner and the bedtime top up. You may also want to push the time for bedtime top up back a bit too, although not necessary.

- If 12:00 a.m. feeding is dropped but baby is waking up an hour early for breakfast, try to push the bedtime top up and 9:00 p.m. feedings back (to 7:30 or 8:00 p.m. for the top up), then feed around 9:30 or 10:00 p.m.

- If baby wakes earlier than 5:00 a.m., treat the feeding like it is a night feeding and push back breakfast to 6:30 a.m. or 7:00 a.m. Then adjust schedule slightly for the day until you are back on track which should be possible to do by mid or end of the day.

- Watch for habits. If this midnight feeding is dropped but baby is waking before 5:00 a.m. on a regular basis, they may not be ready – start feeding them at midnight again for a few days to re–establish the routine before you try again. Consistency is important.

Phase 4: Week 12 (three months) on – sleep through the night

This phase is generally the same as the prior stage except that you have the option of dropping the 9:00 p.m. feeding so baby sleeps a minimum of 10 hours uninterrupted.* Be patient with your baby and make sure they are ready before you drop this feeding – make sure baby has had a consistent routine for at least a week or two. You should have more flexibility in terms of your schedule but consistency is still important.

Phase 4 suggested schedule

6:00 a.m. – breakfast time feeding, same as above

9:00 a.m. – morning feeding time, same as above

12:00 p.m. – lunch time feeding, same as above

3:00 p.m. – afternoon feeding time, same as above

6:00 p.m. – dinner time feeding (bedtime top up), same as above

9:00 p.m. – optional night feed (temporary, sleepsack/swaddle on)*

*This 9:00 p.m. feeding will be the same as above until you are ready to drop this feeding. We do not recommend dropping this feeding unless baby's schedule has been consistent for a few weeks since dropping the midnight feeding. Refer to tips below.

Note: Refer to the sample baby charts for each phase below.

Bedtime top up to help your baby through the night

From the time your baby starts to sleep through the night until they are a year old, consider always topping up with breastmilk or formula before bedtime, or giving them a snack before bed (if they are already eating solids). This is probably as much of a *dream feed* as you should need if you've been using our schedule.

When offering an evening snack to children, try to avoid foods that contain caffeine (such as pop and chocolate) as well as foods that are high in sugar – try to avoid foods with these ingredients generally, which you can read more about on our site, including tips for reducing sugar. An apple and cheese or some plain yogurt with banana will assist in preparing your little one's body for rest. If tolerated, whole dairy is a good option because it contains tryptophan and carbohydrate. For more on this, visit our site and Calmmother contributor Michael Ofer's site (www.michalofer.com).

Your baby may begin to eat so much solid food at dinner that they will not have much breastmilk or formula then, and only have breastmilk or formula at the top up (or evening snack) before bed. Below we discuss replacing the bedtime bottles around the one year mark to assist with less liquids before bed to assist with potty training.

If your baby has been consistently having whole feedings during the day and sleeping 10 to 12 hours at night, and then starts waking up early for breakfast (or waking up hungry in the middle of the night), they may not be getting enough calories and nutrients during the day to carry them through the night.

Consult with your healthcare provider about introducing solids or at least adding a scoop of cereal to your baby's bedtime bottle if you are bottle feeding. Note that this makes breastmilk or formula thicker, and may require use of a larger (or Y shaped) nipple.

Keep in mind that adding cereal to your baby's bottle on a regular basis is not recommended as it may be more difficult to cut out the bedtime snack after a year if they are relying on the bottle for heartiness rather than eating enough during the day. Refer to the Ask Dr. Pam Q&A on our site to find out how to know if your baby is getting enough nutrients.

Tips for Phase 4 3 to 6 months (gentle, patient, persistent & consistent)

Feeding tips for 3 to 6 months

- Refer to the above tips as they are still applicable.
- Baby should be able to stay awake for longer periods of time and may even be ready to drop a nap during the day, though not recommended. See below for more information about dropping naps.
- Baby may take a whole feeding quicker now – if possible, try to shorten the feeding window to half an hour, maximum an hour. Continue to establish clear feeding windows, play time as well as nap and bed times.
- If baby isn't ready to eat at feeding time or if they need a break during, which sometimes happens, it can still take 1.5 hours to feed them. This may be because baby gets distracted easily at this stage. Continue to try feeding them every 15 minutes, repeating if necessary.
- During the day, if baby is awake and it's too early to feed them or if they are not ready yet, let them play before feeding. Always let them play afterward, even if only for 5 minutes.
- Baby should be used to their routine by now and know what time it is.

Sleep tips for 3 to 6 months

- Wait at least 5 minutes after feeding before putting baby down in sleepsack, especially if it's during the day (play time). Baby should be awake when you put them down. Continue to tell them what time it is.
- At night feedings, feed in dimly lit, quiet room and whispering to help teach baby night time (sleepsack on, no play – snuggles only!).
- Each sleep time should be 1.5 to 3 hours (1.5 to 2 hours is optimal).
- Always make sure baby has a fully tummy, had a burp after their feeding, a clean diaper and is comfortable before you put them down.

Tips for dropping the 9:00 p.m. feeding

- Do not drop this feeding unless baby's schedule has been consistent for a few weeks since dropping the midnight feeding. Ideally, baby is sleeping so well at this point that you either have to wake them for breakfast, or they wake up cooing rather than starving.
- If this 9:00 p.m. feeding is dropped but baby is waking up an hour early hungry for breakfast (which is not uncommon at first when you drop the 9:00 p.m. feeding), you could try to push the bedtime top up back a bit to 7:30 p.m. or 8:00 p.m. but is not necessary.
- If baby wakes up earlier than 5:00 a.m., treat the feeding like it is a night feeding and push breakfast to 6:30 a.m. or 7:00 a.m. Then adjust schedule slightly for the rest of the day until you are back on track.
- Watch for habits. If this 9:00 p.m. feeding is dropped but baby is waking before 5:00 a.m. on a regular basis, they may not be ready – start feeding at 9:00 p.m. for a few days to re-establish the routine.
- After 4 months, if baby has been sleeping consistently through the night then begins to wake hungry in the night or early in the morning, consult with your healthcare provider about introducing solids.

Six to 12 months: Solids – maintain sleeping through the night

This phase is the same as the prior stage except for the introduction of solids. You may notice that your baby will consistently sleep 11 or 12 hours uninterrupted at this point, especially if they are being fed solids. A consistent routine is still important but your schedule should be more flexible. *Note that milk means breastmilk or formula unless baby's healthcare provider advises baby should drink anything else.

Six to 12 months suggested schedule

6:00 a.m. – breakfast time
- Wake up. Start feeding between 5:00 a.m. and 7:00 a.m.
- Feed solids first then milk* for ½ an hour to an hour

9:00 a.m. – morning snack
- Wake up. Start feeding between 8:00 a.m. and 10:00 a.m.
- Feed solids and milk for ½ an hour to an hour

12:00 p.m. – lunch time
- Wake up. Start feeding between 11:00 a.m. and 1:00 p.m.
- Feed solids then milk for ½ an hour to an hour

3:00 p.m. – afternoon snack
- Wake up. Start feeding between 2:00 p.m. and 4:00 p.m.
- Feed solids and milk for ½ an hour to an hour

6:00 p.m. – dinner time (and bedtime top up)
- Wake up. Start feeding solids then milk between 5:30 p.m. and 6:30 p.m. for ½ hour up to an hour
- Bedtime routine (brush gums and teeth, bath or wash face, story, etc.)
- Top baby up with breastmilk or formula 15 minutes before bedtime

Note: Refer to the sample baby charts for each phase below.

Tips for six to 12 months (continue to ensure consistency)

Feeding tips for six to 12 months (refer to the above tips as they still apply)

- Baby should be able to stay awake for longer periods of time and may even be ready to start dropping a nap during the day.
- Baby may only take half an hour to an hour to have a whole feeding now, but may get distracted more easily. Continue to establish clear feeding windows, and try to shorten the window to half an hour maximum an hour if possible.
- If baby isn't ready to eat at feeding time or if they need a break during, it can still take 1.5 hours feed them (just milk after the hour point) – if so, continue to try feeding them every 15 minutes.
- During the day, if baby is awake and it's too early to feed them or if not ready, let them play before feeding. Always let them play afterward, even if only for 5-10.

Sleep tips for six to 12 months (ideally baby falls asleep while awake on their own)

- Wait 5-30 minutes after feeding before putting baby down in sleepsack.
- Baby should be awake when you put them down to sleep. Continue to tell them what time it is (i.e., it's nap time, play time, or bedtime, etc.).
- Although the bedtime feeding is a top up, the more you can feed baby before bedtime the better, especially now that they are sleeping through the night. When baby has had as much as you think they will eat and drink at dinner and needs a break, continue on with their bedtime routine – they will probably drink a bit extra at the bedtime top up. You also may find that it may make sense to start feeding baby dinner half an hour earlier to create a bigger spread between dinner and the bedtime top up. You may also want to push the time for bedtime top up back a bit as well. Adjust a bit so that it works for you.
- If baby is waking up an hour early for breakfast, you could try to push the bedtime top up back to 7:30 p.m. or 8:00 p.m. (not necessary as long as tummy is full).
- If baby wakes up earlier than 5:00 a.m. to eat, treat it like a night feeding and push back breakfast to 6:30 or 7:00 a.m. Adjust your schedule accordingly for the day.
- If baby is waking before 5:00 a.m. to eat on a regular basis, they may not be eating enough in the day (it may be time for solids, consult physician).
- Each nap should be 1.5 to 3 hours in length (1.5 to 2 hours is optimal), ideally laying down rather than on you for majority of the sleep.
- Always make sure baby has a full tummy, is well burped and is comfy (clean diaper, etc.) before you put them down for a nap or bedtime.

Other important things

In addition to the things we've already discussed, there are lots of other topics that may become relevant for families at different times. We have highlighted some below. Visit our site for more tips and information.

Feeding and sleep one year onward

When it comes to feeding and sleep, this phase is pretty much the same as the last six months because your baby is consistently sleeping through the night uninterrupted. Consistency in your routine is still important as you move from the baby phase into the toddler phase, although your schedule should be quite a bit more flexible by now.

Weaning from a bottle (and pacifier)

There may be a few changes with feedings at this stage. You will likely be introducing more, and a variety of, solids. You may also begin to introduce different types of milk if you haven't already (goat, cow, hemp, oat, rice, almond, cashew etc.). Check out our homemade hemp recipe on our site. You may also begin to phase out baby bottles if you were using them with your baby. Instead of a bedtime bottle, you may eventually offer a bedtime snack of some sort.

There is no magic or even any rush to start weaning a baby from their bottle. From a practical perspective, the sooner you can get rid of a toddler's bottles and diapers the better, if it makes life easier. And one of the main reasons for transitioning away from drinking liquids before bed is that our potty training method begins as early as 18 months and involves getting rid of diapers completely at that time. This is why the bedtime feeding is described above as being a *top up* rather than a separate feeding (and why we mention a bedtime bottle can be replaced by a bedtime snack).

Even at five or six months of age an infant can start to learn the coordination to drink out of a regular cup. The tongue-thrust reflex starts to diminish by their first birthday and this is when they will be able to get a better lip seal around a cup – prior to this time a sippy-cup maybe a cleaner option.

Consider starting to wean your baby from their bedtime feeding between 12 to 14 months. Depending on your preference, you could make the transition from a bottle to a soft sippy cup, particularly for the bedtime feeding. Make this transition slowly to avoid stressing your baby out especially if you have a well established bedtime routine that involves breastfeeding or a bottle. Refer to the posts on our site for more.

Tips for dropping naps during the day

There is no reason to rush dropping naps. Your child may continue to have a nap each day after lunch until they are three or even four years old (or beyond). Your child may need a half hour to three hour nap each day (or every few days, and eventually on weekends only) until they are in grade school.

There are so many health benefits associated with sleep and napping. At minimum, dropping naps too early could risk throwing off the ability to sleep through the night (if they're too overtired, they may not be able to fall or stay asleep).

We generally do not recommend dropping any naps during the day until baby is consistently sleeping through the night for at least a month.

Our suggestions for dropping naps are below but one reason you might want to drop a nap is if you really feel that your baby is getting too much sleep during the day and that it is hindering their ability to sleep through the night – if so, try dropping the late afternoon nap first. Consistently skipping naps or having an earlier or later bedtime may create a habit for your baby over time.

The amount of sleep that each baby needs in a day will vary. Below are a few suggestions to consider when it comes to naps. It is not a coincidence that the times below are consistent with when many daycares have nap time. Convenience and ease are our priority. Find out more tips about babies, naps and sleep on our site.

- Baby naps a minimum of 1.5 hours between each daytime feeding until they are at least six months old. This means four naps a day:
    - early morning after the breakfast time feeding
    - late morning after the morning snack time feed
    - early afternoon after the lunchtime feed, and
    - late afternoon after the afternoon snack feed.

- Drop the late afternoon nap before dinner around six months, preferably after they are consistently sleep through the night.

- Drop the late morning nap around nine months or when ready. When you drop this nap, your baby may need to have two naps during the day, in the morning after breakfast and after lunch, for 1.5 to three hours each nap.

- Drop the early morning nap after breakfast when your baby is around a year old, and continues to have a 1.5 to three hour nap after lunch.

Baby essentials and safety

The information is below. Print the checklists directly from our site!

Baby essentials (0 to four months)

Baby basics

- Government certified car seat
- Stroller complete with all the attachments you need (i.e., attachment for car seat, extra seat or skateboard for kids, etc.)
- Diaper bag (see checklist below)

Nice-to-have basics

- Seat protector to protect seat cushions
- Car seat case – helpful for travelling and helps prevent damaging to car seat when placed with checked luggage
- Head hugger to keep baby's head in place while in car seat
- Baby carrier
- Travel crib with two waterproof mattress covers and two sheets (playpens are typically heavier and less versatile but they are also generally less expensive)

Nursery furniture

- Government certified crib with mattress, two waterproof mattress covers and two bottom sheets (consider a bassinet or convertibility/extension kit option, depending on your preference)
- Mobile for above crib
- Change table, pad and two covers
- Baby monitor (the camera's are super helpful for ease of checking on baby, including for sleep training purposes)
- Rocking chair and baby swing are luxury items

For your baby's bottom

- Diapers - before buying in bulk, consider trying a few brands to find what you like
- Small pack of Newborn (up to about 10 lbs)
- Small pack of smallest size (usually 8-15 pounds)
- Wipes (wiper warmer is a luxury)
- Bum balm, preferably petroleum free (preventative, to be used with each change, particularly during first 24 hours while poop is black)
- Diaper rash cream, preferably petroleum free
- Diaper bin with sealed cover and bags

Baby clothes (minimum amount recommended)*

- 3-4 swaddle blankets
- Sleep sacs
- 2 sleep sacs with swaddle – for when baby transitions from swaddle to sleep sac (you may want to try one first as you may be able to put baby directly into a sleep sac without a swaddle)
- 2 sleep sacs without swaddle
- 6 cotton onesies/sleepers, preferably with a zippers (buttons and clasps can get annoying to do up especially in middle of the night!)
- 4 cotton shirts/sweater and pant sets for putting over onesies
- 6 pairs of cotton socks
- 2 cotton baby hats
- 6 pairs of cotton scratch mittens
- 1 pair of baby shoes or booties
- 3 drool bibs for when bay starts to teeth
- 3 Pee-Pee Teepees to cover up boys private parts while you are changing them, optional

* Depending on the size of your baby, newborn sizes may end up being too small within a week or two, so you may want to consider buying fewer newborn sizes and more 0-3 months as cotton tends to shrink!

Seasonal items

- Cooler temperatures
- Bunting bag or snow suit
- Toque, mittens and baby boots
- Accessories for stroller such as waterproof weather/dust cover
- Car seat cover for winter – great for avoiding having to put extra layers on baby as well as travelling
- Warmer temperatures
- Sun hat
- Accessories for stroller – sun cover and bug canopy
- Sunscreen safe for babies, when old enough

Hygiene and bath time

- Baby bath tub
- 8-10 baby facecloths (or baby sponge if preferred)
- 2 bath towels, preferably with hood
- Hair and body wash
- Oil (olive, coconut or other preferred oil) and/or lotion
- Baby hair brush
- Baby oil and small comb (to be prepared for Cradle Cap)
- Baby nail clippers and file kit

Baby toys

- Baby swing or chair
- Activity gym
- Teething toy
- Toy basket(s) to help keep things organized
- Play mats (if your floor is hard and/or to protects rugs)
- Hard baby book(s)

Breastfeeding/expressing

- Nursing cover
- Breastfeeding pillow and 2 pillowcases
- Breast pump and paraphenelia
- Bottles for pump
- Breast milk freezer bags or silicon ice cube tray (to freeze breast milk and the transfer to plastic bags in freezer)
- Glass bottles
- Nipples for bottle (slow to fast flow - note that formula tends to be thicker than breastmilk)
- Bottle brush
- Bottle drying rack
- Bottle steam sterilizer
- Microwave steam sterilizer bags for pump and bottles (on the go)
- Portable cool bottle holder case with ice packs
- Bottle warmer (and one portable bottle warmer as well)
- 15 bibs (and baby facecloths are also helpful)
- 15 burping blankets
- Formula (always have on hand just in case!)

Formula feeding

- Formula, obviously :)
- Glass bottles and nipples (quicker flow may be necessary as formula tends to be thicker than breastmilk)
- Bottle brush
- Bottle drying rack
- Bottle steam sterilizer
- Microwave steam sterilizer bags (for on the go)
- Portable cool bottle holder case with ice packs
- Bottle warmer (and one portable bottle warmer as well)
- 15 bibs (and baby facecloths are also helpful)
- 15 burping blankets

Vitamins and medicinal type basics to have on hand**

- Soother and clip
- Teething jewellery for Mom to wear
- Amber teething necklace for baby
- Vitamins
- Liquid Vitamin D
- Liquid Probiotic
- Thermometer
- Baby nasal aspirator
- Homeopathics and traditional medicine (some mentioned above)
    - Camilia - for teething
    - Windi - for gas and colic relief
    - Coryzalia - for cold prevention
    - Oscillococcinum - for flu prevention
    - Quietude - for restlessness and disorders associated with restlessness such as irritability and mild sleeping disorders (occasional sleeplessness, nightmares and night terrors)
    - Thuja Occidentalis - for offsetting side effects of immunizations
    - Belladonna and Ferrum Phosphoricum - for fevers
    - Baby Tylenol

** Consult with your baby's qualified healthcare provider about these medicinal basics prior to giving them to your baby.

Baby essentials (4-6 months onward)

Feeding

- High chair/seat when solids are introduced and baby can sit up
- Bibs that are easy to wipe down!
- Facecloths
- Fresh food for introducing whole foods to babies and toddlers
- Baby bowls and plate, and spoons (with long handles is easier)
- Sippy cup and regular cup, as appropriate
- Fork and spoon, as appropriate
- Baby food paraphernalia
- Drool bibs for when baby is teething

Playtime

- Baby fold-away jumper or Jolly Jumper
- Baby seat or chair
- Baby activity table (to practice standing)
- Teething toys
- Stuffed animals
- Board books

Confirm current government safety standards for when it is considered safe both from a height and age perspective to put your child in a forward facing car seat and eventually a booster seat.

Your diaper bag

A well-equipped diaper bag can be the difference between a pleasant outing and a potentially disastrous one. As a general rule of thumb – it is best to be over prepared. You can never predict what is going to happen or how equipped the space is that you find yourself in. Trying to remember everything can be challenging. You often find gaps in your packing at the most inopportune time (when things have gone sideways). To help in this process, here is a list of "must haves" and some "nice haves" compiled by experienced Moms who have learned from a few disastrous experiences of their own! This list will vary according to weather as well as the age of your child.

Must haves

- Diapers – for new babies, pack at least one for every hour you plan to be away plus a couple extra
- Wipes – if you don't have a reusable package (highly recommended), throw some into a Ziploc bag
- Wet bag (or large Ziploc bag if you are careful to keep to away from children) for holding dirty diapers or wet/soiled clothing
- Hand sanitizer
- Diaper rash cream
- A folding change pad or blanket (many diaper change travel kits come with wipes case)
- Change of clothes for child - for a baby consider a onesie or a sleeper and for older children a shirt/bottoms
- Change of clothes for you - a shirt is ideal but at the very least a scarf to cover up any mishaps
- Bib
- Tissues
- Receiving blankets
- Soother/teething toys
- Required medication
- Phone, keys and wallet (a handful of change in bag at all times)

Feeding things

- Baby food/healthy snacks
- Spoon, bowl, bag for empty dirty dishes
- Snack trap for finger foods
- Sippy cup (if applicable)
- Bottle fed babies
- Clean bottles
- Bottles of water and powdered formula (try formula dispensers like Munchkin Formula Dispenser Combo Pack). While more expensive, premixed formula is super convenient when out and about
- Breast fed babies
- Expressed breast milk (this will require a cooling device)
- A nursing cover or blanket should you choose
- A few nursing pads and nipple cream
- Food and drink for you

Nice haves

- Insulated bottle tote/heater
- Pacifier holder you can clip onto stroller
- Stain eraser or tide on the go
- Face clothes
- Nail clippers/file
- Lip balm/gloss
- Hair ties
- Sling if your little one gets fussy and wants out of stroller
- Disposable changing sheet (one less thing for you to wash)
- Grocery cart cover
- Bag for scrapes and cuts (Band-Aids/ointment)
- Cell phone charger
- Toys (that are in one piece and not too small)
- Books (a great idea especially the interactive kind)

Weather dependent

- Sunscreen
- Sunglasses
- Hat
- Mitts

Once you are home and have a moment to breathe, replace items used so your bag is set and ready to go for the next outing!

Great tip: Keep a backup supply of diapers, wipes, a change of clothes, socks, water and non-perishable snacks (like trail mix) in your vehicle. This has saved us more than once!

Baby proofing your home

Preparing your house for the arrival of your baby can seem like a daunting task. You only need to crawl around on your hands and knees for a few minutes to see all the potential dangers that exist. We cannot possibly protect our kids from every bump and bruise, despite our best efforts, but thoroughly baby proofing your house can greatly reduce the risk of serious injury.

While your eagle-eyes are by far the best baby proofing you can do, don't underestimate how tired you are likely to feel the first year and how quickly things can happen. What should you do before baby arrives and what can wait until they show signs they are ready to crawl? Here is a list of ideas to get you started.

Baby proofing things to consider before your baby arrives

General

- Have a working carbon monoxide detector
- Ensure all fire detectors are operating
- Stock your first aid kit
- Have emergency numbers easily accessible
- Remove all poisonous plants or keep them out of reach
- Make sure small choking hazards are out of reach (as a general rule, anything that can fit inside a toilet paper roll is a hazard!)

Baby room

- Ensure your crib meets federal safety standards
- Have a firm mattress that fits the frame
- Do not place crib in front of window, heat register, decorations, or anything that baby can grab
- Avoid bumper pads on crib
- Do not leave toys, puffy blankets or pillows in the child's crib (consider putting baby to sleep in a secure swaddle or sleep sack)
- If using a change table, ensure it has raised edges and a safety strap (note - the safest place to change a baby is on the floor)
- Consider a baby monitor with video so you can check on them regularly but make sure the cord is secure and out of baby's reach

Bathroom

- Have an anti-slip bath mat (do not use a bath seat to prop baby up)
- Adjust thermostat to monitor hot water temperature, below 120 degrees Fahrenheit (48.89 degrees Celsius), to avoid scalding
- Preparing for movement (on average between six to 10 months)

Baby room

- Ensure all large furniture pieces that can topple are bolted to the wall with furniture straps
- Avoid placing furniture that child can climb in front of window/ledge
- Do not trust that a screen will protect your child from a fall! If you do want to open the window, consider window stops or guards that restrict how far it can open (these apparatuses should be strong enough to prevent your toddler from removing but easy for you to remove in the event of a fire)
- Keep baby toiletries out of reach, including baby wipes
- Cover all electrical outlets that are not kid safe and remove all wires or appliances that plug in

Bathroom

- Remove water as soon as bath is done
- Ensure all vitamins, medications and other poisonous items are secure in medicine cabinet
- Keep all makeup, razors, pins, perfume, mouthwash, nail polish and remover, scissors or other harmful objects out of reach
- Keep the toilet seat down or latched (or keep bathroom door shut)
- Invest in a bathtub spout
- Clean bath toys regularly with vinegar and warm water to avoid mildew and mold, especially inside squeeze toys

Kitchen

- When you can, cook on back burners with pot handles facing back of stove
- Secure oven door with a clamp
- Put a latch on drawers containing knives or other sharp objects
- Household cleaning items (including dishwasher tabs) should be placed out of reach
- Unplug kitchen appliances that sit on the counter and don't keep cords dangling
- Be aware of food in the fridge or pantry that your child may have access to and place out of reach
- Keep hot food and drink away from table/counter edges and refrain from holding while baby is in your arms
- Avoid table cloths or runners that can be pulled down
- Have a safe and sturdy highchair with a working safety belt, and if you transition to a booster seat when your baby is older, make sure it also has a working seat belt

Various other rooms

- Remove small choking hazards (as a general rule, anything that can fit inside a toilet paper roll is a choking hazard)
- Secure all large furniture pieces, like bookshelves and televisions, to the wall
- Install baby gates to keep child away from hazardous areas
- Cover all sharp corners with edge guards
- Tie, bind or remove all dangling cords on window covers
- Tie up all electrical wires or keep out of reach
- Remove lamps that can topple and secure all cords
- Cover all electrical outlets that are not kid safe
- Avoid placing breakable items within reach, including picture frames
- Use door stops to protect fingers
- Use door knob covers to keep selected rooms off limits
- Blow out the pilot light to your electrical fireplace or install a fireplace grill
- Use child-resistant covers if you have accessible garbage cans
- Safely store all plastic bags and balloons
- Safely store batteries, matches and lighters
- All guns and ammunition should be removed from house or safely locked up

Check your backyard, garage and vehicle for safety hazards, including making sure your child safety door and window locks are on when driving! Never leave your baby or child unsupervised.

Toddler proofing your home

Watching your little one progress from crawling to walking is a milestone to be celebrated. The world suddenly opens up and within it are a plethora of things to grab, climb on and stick in your mouth!

Toddlers are naturally curious, adventurous and depending on their age, can be a little bit sneaky. In other words, this is not the time to let up on childproofing your home! The older children get the higher they can climb to reach the things they want to get their hands on.

Your child's age, their abilities and their temperament can help determine the extent of proofing you may require. While your parenting style and comfort level will also guide you, keep in mind that the single leading cause of death in children over one is unintentional injury, many of which are preventable.

While you can't prevent all accidents from happening, there are things you can do around your home to help keep your toddler safer. The list of common hazards to watch out for are on our site.

Potty training

If there is one thing we have learned about potty training, it is that there are no set rules!

Children show signs of readiness at different ages and a method that yields great results with one child can be completely ineffective for another, even siblings.

That being said, the methods we believe are most effective are used after children are 18 months old and showing signs of readiness.

Consider starting to phase the bedtime top up bottle out completely anytime after 13 months to ensure you are ready to go with potty training when your little one is.

The Calm potty training method available on our site is a straightforward, relaxed, child-led approach to potty training that allows you to effectively train your child how to use the potty stress-free.

This method is great because you can go about your day almost completely as usual because the potty is always close by your child (which helps to prevent accidents). If you need or want to go out with your child during the potty training process, just put their pull-up diaper or training pants on, and go.

Discipline and conscious parenting

Clearly behavioural concerns are not an issue when it comes to babies but we believe that good communication with your baby is essential from day one. Communication is an intrinsic aspect of our feeding and sleep program. Since effective communication makes life easier with children, we want to briefly touch on this topic.

In the same way we like to combine science-based natural medicine with conventional medical therapeutics at Calmmother.com, so that parents can make informed decisions about health for their families and to benefit from the best of all worlds, we appreciate Dr. Shefali's notion of conscious parenting and this world-renowned clinical psychologist's approach to integrating Eastern philosophy and Western psychology. It applies to families with children of all ages. We believe in the importance of honouring our child's natural state of being, as well as that of others and our own.

We know there are mixed views on disciplining children. Thankfully physical and fear-based discipline ideologies have all but disappeared. Behavioral concerns can often be monitored or mitigated by parents, especially if they involve things like escalated energy levels (hyper from being on a sugar high or just over excited generally) or from being hungry (or even hangry), or tired (sleepy or crashing from a sugar high). Challenging behaviour can be caused by a desire for attention, lack of awareness and communication between parent and child, and then there's curiosity and mischievousness.

As parents we never never intentionally want to break our child's spirit!

Our *timeout bubble* approach, which essentially facilitates self-reflection and being aware/conscious of our actions, is about our actions, is as close as it gets to disciplining toddlers and preschool aged children for us. It is focused on facilitating healthy communication, empowers children and parents, and helps to gently diffuse heated situations. And it is also super convenient for parents because the bubble is portable to anywhere you and your child are.

To make things fair, anyone in the family can be put into timeout bubble for something they have said or done. For example, parents can put themselves into, or be put into a timeout bubble by their children, for saying bad words. Essentially the timeout bubble puts you into a place of self reflection in terms of what you've done (or what you have said) and how you maybe would have preferred to have acted (what you should have said) in hindsight, and how to make the situation better (with an apology, and perhaps communicating to the person you may have offended by telling them how they made you feel, rather than choosing to lash out at them). These are the types of things you speak about with your child when someone in the family is in a timeout bubble. Since a timeout bubble follows you around everywhere, even if you go for quiet time in your room to cool off and reflect by yourself, it remains until you all agree the timeout bubble should be *popped* to let you out. Consider no playtime or electronic device time until you are out of the timeout bubble. Also consider no talking to anyone unless it is to discuss the situation and make an apology.

As children get older, family discussions and taking things away tends to be more effective way for curbing unacceptable behaviour. Check out our site for more tips and ideas relating to a variety of topics about children, including discipline, exercise, and mindfulness, meditation and manifesting.

Finding the right childcare for your family

Deciding who will care for your child can be heart wrenching!

Finding the right childcare provider can be very stressful and often takes a significant amount of time and energy.

Only you will be able to decide whether it's best for you to stay at home to care for your baby, or return to work after your baby is born – whether it's immediately following delivery, after maternity leave, or when your child is older. Depending on the age of your child (or children) and financial circumstances, it may be best for your family to hire a nanny, or take your child to a day home or daycare. Sharing a nanny with another family may also be a good option, especially if you each have one child or if you only require part time care.

Our guide to childcare on our site outlines important considerations to help you make more informed childcare decisions for you and your family. From a list of interview questions to a form of nanny contract, we've got you covered.

Closing

We are beyond grateful to be on this journey through parenthood with you!

We believe a full night of sleep for Mothers and their families will change the world.

It is our sincere hope that this book helps you simplify life so you can focus on what matters most to you, or that you have found at least one aspect of value.

Share the link to our site and this program with your fellow parents. Also connect with us on social media and on YouTube, and let us know what you've found most valuable about this program by leaving comments!

Your feedback is what helps us continue to create helpful content to support other parents and their families.

In health, and with much love and gratitude,

Tereza and Dr. Pam

Notes & supplemental documents

[1] Michael H Bonnet, and Donna L. Arand. 1995. *We are Chronically Sleep Deprived, American Sleep Disorders Association and Sleep Research Society.* Sleep: 18(10):908-11. Available at: https://www.researchgate.net/publication/14456961_We_are_Chronically_Sleep_Deprive d.

[2] David Richter, et al. 2019. *Long-term effects of pregnancy and childbirth on sleep satisfaction and duration of first-time and experienced mothers and fathers.* Sleep: Volume 42, Issue 4. Available at: https://academic.oup.com/sleep/article/42/4/zsz015/5289255. Study also discussed at https://www.theguardian.com/lifeandstyle/2019/feb/26/parenthood-sleep-deprivation-aft er-birth-mothers-hit-hardest-research.

[3] Wolfsen, A., A. Futterman, and P. Lacks. 1992. *Effects of parent training on infant sleep patterns, parent's stress, and parental perceived competency.* Journal of Consulting and Clinical Psychology: 60(1) 41-48.

[4] We found a number of aspects of *On Becoming Baby Wise: Giving Your Infant the Gift of Nighttime Sleep* by Gary Ezzo and Robert Bucknam M.D. (Parent-Wise Solutions, Inc.; Rev Upd edition (Feb. 1 2012) (Babywise) useful in principle. Same with the Ferber method. There are many differences between our feeding and sleep program and Babywise method, however we believe that our program does apply certain ideas introduced in Babywise. Most importantly, Babywise provides a very helpful timeline in terms of when it is appropriate to cut out certain feedings to help ensure your baby sleeps through the night at three months - thank you Babywise! Other concepts introduced in Babywise we think are important include the notion of *whole feedings* and consistently feeding breakfast at the same time every day. Dr. Pam and other healthcare providers have also made similar recommendations, including feeding newborns approximately every three hours around the clock and try to always feed them whole feedings each time. Always consult your healthcare provider about your baby.

[5] Bayol, et al., 2008. *Offspring from mothers fed a 'junk food' diet in pregnancy and lactation exhibit exacerbated adiposity that is more pronounced in females.* The Journal of Physiology: 586 (Pt 13): 3219–3230. Available at: https://www.ncbi.nlm.nih.gov/pmc/articles/PMC2538787/.

[6] George Du Toit, M.B., B.Ch., et al. *Randomized Trial of Peanut Consumption in Infants at Risk for Peanut Allergy.* The New England Journal of Medicine: February 26, 2015 Available at: http://www.nejm.org/doi/full/10.1056/NEJMoa1414850?.2015 study showed a significant reduction in peanut allergy in children when they were exposed to peanuts between four and seven months old.

[7] Dr. Harvey Karp, *The Happiest Baby*. Available at: https://www.happiestbaby.com/blogs/baby/the-5-s-s-for-soothing-babies.

Blank chart for your baby

Download this chart on our website for free to use with your baby.

Sample baby charts for each phase

Sample Chart – 2014   *Calmmother Method*
                                     Weeks 3–7

Name: Baby No. of wks: 3 Month/date: Jan	Monday 14	Tuesday 15	Wednesday 16	Thursday 17	Friday 18	Saturday 19	Sunday 20
6:00 – 6:30 am	R15 ptp	L15 ptp	R15 pee	L15 pee	R15 pee	L15 pee	R15 pee
6:30 – 7:00 am	L15	R15	L15	R15	L15	R15	L15
7:00 – 7:30 am	S (2hrs)	A	A	A	S (2hrs)	S (2hrs)	S (2hrs)
7:30 – 8:00 am		S (1.5hrs)	S (1.5hrs)	S (1.5hrs)			
8:00 – 8:30 am							
8:30 – 9:00 am	↓	↓	↓	↓	↓	↓	↓
9:00 – 9:30 am	L15 pee	R15 ptp	L15 pee	R15 pee	L15 D+pee	R15 pee	L15 pee
9:30 – 10:00 am	R15 (M)	L15	R15	L15	R15	L15	R15
10:00 – 10:30 am	A (C)	S (2hrs)	S (2hrs)	A (E)	A	A (E)	A
10:30 – 11:00 am	S (1.5hrs)			S (1.5hrs)	S (1.5hrs)		S (2hrs)
11:00 – 11:30 am							
11:30 – 12:00 pm	↓	↓	↓	↓	↓	↓	↓
12:00 – 12:30 pm	L10 D	R15 D	L15 D	R15 D	L15 D	R15 D	L15 D
12:30 – 1:00 pm	R20 pee	L15 ptp	R15 ptp	L15	R15 pee	L15	R15 ptp
1:00 – 1:30 pm	A (C)	S (2hrs)	A	S (2hrs) F	A	S (2hrs)	A
1:30 – 2:00 pm	S (1.5hrs)		S (2hrs) F		S (1.5hrs)		S (1.5hrs)
2:00 – 2:30 pm							
2:30 – 3:00 pm	↓	↓	↓	↓	↓	↓	↓
3:00 – 3:30 pm	L20 ptp	R20 pee	L20	R20	L20 pee	R20 pee	L20
3:30 – 4:00 pm	R20	L20	R20	L20	R20	L20	R20 pee
4:00 – 4:30 pm	A						
4:30 – 5:00 pm	S (1.5hrs)	S (2hrs)	S (1.5hrs)	S (1.5hrs)			
5:00 – 5:30 pm							
5:30 – 6:00 pm							
6:00 – 6:30 pm	L10 (B)	R15 (B)	L20 (B)	R15 (B)	L10 (B)	R20 (B)	L15 (B)
6:30 – 7:00 pm	R15	L10 pee	R20 pee	L10 pee	R15	R15 pee	L20 ptp
7:00 – 7:30 pm	L5 R5 ooo	L5 R5			L5 R5	pee L5 R5	R5 L5
7:30 – 8:00 pm	S (1.5hrs)	S (1.5hrs)	S (1.5hrs)	S (1.5hrs)	S (1.5hrs)	S (1.5hrs)	S (1.5hrs)
8:00 – 9:00 pm							
9:00 – 10:00 pm	L10 R15 pee	R15 L5 pee	L10 R10 pee	R15 L5 pee	L15 R15 pee	L5 R5 pee	L5 R15 pee
10:00 – 11:00 pm	S (2hrs)	S (2hrs)	S (2hrs)	S (2hrs)	S (2hrs)	S (2hrs)	S (2hrs)
11:00 – 12:00 am							
12:00 – 1:00 am	R15 L5 pee	L5 R5 pee	R15 L5 pee	L5 R5 pee	R15 L5 pee	R15 L5 pee	L15 pee
1:00 – 2:00 am	S (3hrs)	S (3hrs)	S (3hrs)	S (2hrs)	S (2hrs)	S (3hrs)	S (3hrs)
2:00 – 3:00 am							
3:00 – 4:00 am				L5 R5 pee			
4:00 – 5:00 am				S (2hrs)			
5:00 – 6:00 am	↓	↓	↓		↓	↓	↓
Total liquids drunk	R110 L100	R115 L110	R115 L115	R115 L110	R135 L125	R115 L120	R115 L120
Total solids eaten							
Total poops	2	2	1	0	1	0	3
Total pees	6	4	5	6	8	7	6
Total sleep (night)	8.5 hrs	8.5 hrs	8.5 hrs	8.5 hrs	7.5 hrs	8.5 hrs	8.5 hrs
Mom sleep (night)	5 hrs	6 hrs	5 hrs	6 hrs	4 hrs	5 hrs	5 hrs

Comments: Dropped 3 a.m. feeding but baby sometimes wakes at 5 or 5:30 a.m. to eat breakfast. Baby 3 weeks on Monday January 20th. Fed exclusively breastmilk (no nipple confusion).

Highlight breakfast time, then highlight every three hours after for the rest of the day. Your night feedings will change over time.
Include certain detailed information in your chart every hour or half hour, as applicable.
- Number of minutes per breast and/or ounces of formula. Also include type of solid or liquid and amount of each (bites/oz).
- If vitamins or medicine is given (eg. "D" - if vitamins d is given to baby or "M" medicine, specifying type in the Notes section).
- When baby poops ("poo"), pees ("pee") or both ("p+p").
- If baby pukes more than just a small spit up, including projectile vomit, include "V".
- During baby's awake time, insert "A". If applicable, add "(F)" if she is fussing, "(C)" if crying, or "(S)" if asleep at that time.
  Also insert specific activity, such as "(B)" for bath time, "(P)" for play time, "S" for story time, "(O)" for outing, or "(W)" for a walk.
- When you put baby down to sleep, insert "S". Add "(F)" if she is fussing, "(C)" if crying, or "(A)" if awake during that time.
Keep track of the total amount of solids and liquids, poops and pees, and the amount of sleep you and your baby are getting at night.
In the comments section, make a note of observations about your baby (including if crying a lot) and things like date of new foods introduced, etc.

Note tp up before bed.

Chart for Calmmother feeding and sleep method | calmmother.com | Copyright © Calmmother Limited. All rights reserved.

Note: Baby will start having a more regular schedule (hopefully!). And may also sleep longer after midnight until breakfast.

Sample Chart – 2014　　　　　　　　　　　Calmmother Method
　　　　　　　　　　　　　　　　　　　　　Weeks 8–11

Name: Baby	Monday	Tuesday	Wednesday	Thursday	Friday	Saturday	Sunday
No. of wks: 8							
Month/date: Feb	18	19	20	21	22	23	24
6:00 – 6:30 am	R/S	B/S L/S ptp	B/S L/S ptp	B/S L/S prp	S	S	R/S L/S ptp
6:30 – 7:00 am	L/S ptp	A (o)		A (o)	L/S R/S ptp	R/S L/S ptp	S (2.5hrs)
7:00 – 7:30 am	A (o)	S (1.5hrs)	A (n)	S (2hrs)	A (o)	A (o)	
7:30 – 8:00 am	S (1.5hr)		S (1.5hrs)		S (1.5hrs)	S (1.5hr)	
8:00 – 8:30 am							
8:30 – 9:00 am	↓	↓	↓	↓	↓	↓	↓
9:00 – 9:30 am		1oz pee	1oz pee	1oz pee			
9:30 – 10:00 am	3oz pee	1oz	A	S (2hrs)	S (2hrs)	3oz pee	4oz pee
10:00 – 10:30 am	A (B)	A			A	S (2.5hrs)	A
10:30 – 11:00 am	S (1.5hrs)	S (1.5hrs)	S (2hrs)		S (2hrs)		S (1.5hrs)
11:00 – 11:30 am							
11:30 – 12:00 pm	↓	↓	↓	↓	↓	↓	↓
12:00 – 12:30 pm	L/S pee	B/S L/S D	L/S D	L/S D	L/S D	L/S R/S pee	L/S R/S D
12:30 – 1:00 pm	A	ptp	A	pee	R/S	A	pee
1:00 – 1:30 pm		A (2hrs)	A pee	A	D L/S R/S D	A	A (2hrs)
1:30 – 2:00 pm	S (1.5hr)		S (1.5hrs)	S (1.5hrs)	A	S (1.5hrs)	
2:00 – 2:30 pm					S (1.5hrs)		
2:30 – 3:00 pm							
3:00 – 3:30 pm	2oz	2oz pee	3oz pee	2oz pee	2oz	2oz pee	4oz ptp
3:30 – 4:00 pm	A (o) ptp	2oz	A (o)	2oz	2oz ptp	2oz	A
4:00 – 4:30 pm	S (2hrs)	A (n)	S (2hrs)	A (o)	A (o)	A (o)	S (2hrs)
4:30 – 5:00 pm		S (1.5hrs)		S (1.5hrs)	S (1.5hrs)	S (1.5hrs)	
5:00 – 5:30 pm							
5:30 – 6:00 pm	↓	↓	↓	↓	↓	↓	↓
6:00 – 6:30 pm	R/oz pee	R/S ptp	R/o	L/S R/S prp	L/S R/S pee	R/S L/S pee	R/S
6:30 – 7:00 pm	A (B) 1/2oz	L/S (B)	L/S ptp	L/S (B)	L/S (B)	A (B) S	L/S A (B)
7:00 – 7:30 pm	S (2.5hrs) 1oz	1oz		1oz	1oz	2oz	1oz
7:30 – 8:00 pm		S (1.5hrs)	S (1.5hrs)	S (1.5hrs)	S (1.5hrs)	S (1.5hrs)	S (1.5hrs)
8:00 – 9:00 pm							
9:00 – 10:00 pm	↓	↓	↓	↓	↓	↓	↓
10:00 – 11:00 pm	3oz pee	3oz pee	3oz pee	3oz pee	3oz pee	3oz pee	3oz pee
11:00 – 12:00 am	S (7hrs)	S (7.5hrs)	S (7hrs)	S (8hrs)	S (8hrs)	S (7hrs)	S (8hrs)
12:00 – 1:00 am							
1:00 – 2:00 am							
2:00 – 3:00 am							
3:00 – 4:00 am							
4:00 – 5:00 am							
5:00 – 6:00 am							
Total liquids drank	R3.5L 9.5 1oz	L 4.5 L 9.5 1oz	B 10 L 9.5 1oz	R 4.5 L 9.5 3oz	R 4.5 L 9.5 10oz	R 5 L 9 3oz	R 4.5 L 9.5 3oz
Total solids eaten							
Total poops	2	2	2	2	2	2	2
Total pees	6	6	6	6	6	6	6
Total sleep (night)	7 hrs	7.5 hrs	7 hrs	8 hrs	8 hrs	7 hrs	8 hrs
Mom sleep (night)	6 hrs	6.5 hrs	6.5 hrs	7 hrs	7.5 hrs	6 hrs	7 hrs

Comments:
Dropped 12 a.m. feeding but baby sometimes wakes at 5 or 5:30 am to eat breakfast. Baby 8 weeks on Monday February 18th. Fed exclusively breastmilk – bottle + breast.

Highlight breakfast time, then highlight every three hours after for the rest of the day. Your night feedings will change over time.
Include certain detailed information in your chart every hour or half hour, as applicable.
- Number of minutes per breast and/or ounces of formula. Also include type of solid or liquid and amount of each (bites/oz)
- If vitamins or medicine is given (eg. "D" - if vitamin d is given to baby or "M" medicine, specifying type in the Notes section).
- When baby poops ("poo"), pees ("pee") or both ("p+p").
- If baby pukes more than just a small spit up, including projectile vomit, include "V".
- During baby's awake time, insert "A". If applicable, add ("F") if she is fussing, (C) if crying, or (S) if asleep at that time.
  Also insert specific activity, such as (B) for bath time, (P) for play time, (S) for story time, (O) for outing, or (W) for a walk.
- When you put baby down to sleep, insert "S". Add "(F)" if she is fussing, "(C)" if crying, and "(A)" if awake during that time.
Keep track of the total amount of solids and liquids, poops and pees, and the amount of sleep you and your baby are getting at night.
In the comments section, make a note of observations about your baby (including if crying a lot) and things like date of new foods introduced, etc.

Note the top up before bed.

Chart for Calmmother feeding and sleep method | calmmother.com | Copyright © Calmmother Limited. All rights reserved.

Note: Pumping and expressing milk at this point so baby is sometimes breast and other times bottle fed. In this case, mom pumps before bed to keep milk supply.

Sample Chart – 2014 Calmmother Method
Weeks 12 (3mos) – 6 mos

Name: Baby No. of wks: 12 Month/date: Mar	Monday 18	Tuesday 19	Wednesday 20	Thursday 21	Friday 22	Saturday 23	Sunday 24
6:00 – 6:30 am	R/S 4/5 pee	S	S	R/S	L/S R/S pee	S	L/S pee
6:30 – 7:00 am	A (P)	R/S 4/5 p/p		A (P)	A (P)		R/S
7:00 – 7:30 am	S (2 hrs)	A (P)	L/S 4/5 pee	4/5 p/p	↓	R/S 4/5 p/p	A (P)
7:30 – 8:00 am		S (1.5 hrs)	A (P)	A (P)	S (1 hr)	A (P)	S (1.5 hrs)
8:00 – 8:30 am			S (1.5 hrs)	S (1 hr)		S (1.5 hrs)	
8:30 – 9:00 am							
9:00 – 9:30 am	5oz p/p	4oz pee	↓	4oz pee	5oz p/p		4oz p/p
9:30 – 10:00 am	A (W)	3oz	↓	A (P)	A (W)	3oz pee	S (F)
10:00 – 10:30 am	S (C)	A (C)	A (W)		S (F)	A (W)	
10:30 – 11:00 am	(2 hrs)	S (1.5 hrs)	S (2 hrs)	S (1 hr)		S (1.5 hrs)	(1 hr)
11:00 – 11:30 am							
11:30 – 12:00 pm	↓		↓		↓		
12:00 – 12:30 pm	4oz D		4oz D		↓	2oz D	3oz D
12:30 – 1:00 pm	A (P)	4oz D	A (P)	4oz D	4oz D	A (P)	A (P)
1:00 – 1:30 pm	S (2 hrs)	A (W)	S (1.5 hrs)	A (O)	S (1 hr)	S (1 hr)	S (1 hr)
1:30 – 2:00 pm		S (1.5 hrs)		S (1.5 hrs)			
2:00 – 2:30 pm							
2:30 – 3:00 pm	↓		↓		↓		
3:00 – 3:30 pm	4/5 R/S pee	4/5 pee	4/5 pee	4/5 pee	4/5 pee	4/5 pee	4/5 R/S pee
3:30 – 4:00 pm	A (P)	A (P)	R/S	R/S	A (P)	S (2 hrs)	S (2 hrs)
4:00 – 4:30 pm	S (1.5 hrs)	A (P)	A (P)	A (P)	S (1.5 hrs)		
4:30 – 5:00 pm		S (1 hr)	S (1.5 hrs)	S (1 hr)			
5:00 – 5:30 pm							
5:30 – 6:00 pm	2oz p/p	6oz	3oz p/p	2oz p/p	4oz p/p	6oz	6oz p/p
6:00 – 6:30 pm	A (B)	2oz	A (B)	A (B)	A (B)	6oz p/p	A (B)
6:30 – 7:00 pm		A (B)				A (B)	
7:00 – 7:30 pm	↓	4oz	↓	5oz	↓	4oz	4oz
7:30 – 8:00 pm			4oz	S (10.5 hrs)	S (10.5 hrs)	4oz	S (10 hrs)
8:00 – 9:00 pm	S (10 hrs)	S (11 hrs)	S (10 hrs)			S (10 hrs)	
9:00 – 10:00 pm							
10:00 – 11:00 pm							
11:00 – 12:00 am							
12:00 – 1:00 am							
1:00 – 2:00 am							
2:00 – 3:00 am							
3:00 – 4:00 am							
4:00 – 5:00 am	↓	↓	↓	↓	↓	↓	↓
5:00 – 6:00 am							
Total liquids drank	R 30 L 30 14oz	R 20 L 30 4oz	R 20 L 30 13oz	R 30 L 30 12oz	R 30 L 30 11oz	R 30 L 30 16oz	R 30 L 30 14oz
Total solids eaten							
Total poops	2	2	2	2	2	2	2
Total pees	5	5	5	5	5	5	5
Total sleep (night)							
Mom sleep (night)	9 hrs	10 hrs	8 hrs	9 hrs	8 hrs	8 hrs	8 hrs

Comments:
Dropped 9 p.m. feeding but baby sometimes wakes at 5 or 5:30 for breakfast.
Baby 12 weeks on Monday March 18th. Feed exclusively breastmilk – bottle + breast.

Highlight breakfast time, then highlight every three hours after for the rest of the day. Your night feedings will change over time.
Include certain detailed information in your chart every hour or half hour, as applicable.
- Number of minutes per breast and/or ounces of formula. Also include type of solid or liquid and amount of each (bites/oz).
- If vitamins or medicine is given (eg. "D" - if vitamin d is given to baby or "M" medicine, specifying type in the Notes section).
- When baby poops ("poo"), pees ("pee") or both ("p+p").
- If baby pukes more than just a small spit up, including projectile vomit, include "V".
- During baby's awake time, insert "A". If applicable, add "(F)" if she is fussing, "(C)" if crying, or "(S)" if asleep at that time.
  Also insert specific activity, such as "(B)" for bath time, "(P)" for play time, "S" for story time, "(O)" for outing, or "(W)" for a walk.
- When you put baby down to sleep, insert "S". Add "(F)" if she is fussing, "(C)" if crying, or "(A)" if awake during that time.
  Keep track of the total amount of solids and liquids, poops and pees, and the amount of sleep you and your baby are getting at night.
  In the comments section, make a note of observations about your baby (including if crying a lot) and things like date of new foods introduced, etc.

Growth spurt – baby wake up early hungry from a few naps (after an hour).

Chart for Calmmother feeding and sleep method | calmmother.com | Copyright © Calmmother Limited. All rights reserved.

Note slightly earlier dinner and clear top up feed at night before bed.

Sample Chart - 2014
For a 6 month old

Calmmother Method
6 mos - 1 year

Name: Baby No. of wks: 26 Month/date: Jun	Monday 2	Tuesday 3	Wednesday 4	Thursday 5	Friday 6	Saturday 7	Sunday 8
6:00 - 6:30 am	S	L/S R/S pee	L/S R/S 2b	S		R/S p+p	
6:30 - 7:00 am	R/S L/S 2b	R/S 2b	A (W) p+p		R/S 3b	L/S 3b	S
7:00 - 7:30 am	A (W)	A (P) p+p	S (2 hrs)	L/S R/S 5b	L/S	A (P) pee	L/S R/S 5b
7:30 - 8:00 am	S (1.5 hrs)	S (1.5 hrs)		A (O) p+p	A (W) p+p	S (1.5 hrs)	A (W) p+p
8:00 - 8:30 am				S (1.5 hrs)	S (1.5 hrs)		S (1.5 hrs)
8:30 - 9:00 am	↓	↓	↓			↓	
9:00 - 9:30 am	3oz pee 4oz		3oz			3oz p+p	
9:30 - 10:00 am	A (P)	A (P) pee	A (O) pee	↓	↓	A (P)	3oz pee
10:00 - 10:30 am	S (2 hrs)	S (2 hrs)	S (2.5 hrs)	A (W)	A (O) pee	S (2 hrs)	A (P)
10:30 - 11:00 am				S (1.5 hrs)	S (1.5 hrs)		S (1 hr)
11:00 - 11:30 am							
11:30 - 12:00 pm	↓	↓	↓			↓	3oz 3b
12:00 - 12:30 pm	3oz 1b	3oz 1b	3oz 1b	↓	3oz 2b	4oz 2b	A (O) pee
12:30 - 1:00 pm	A (P)	A (P) pee	A (P) p+p	3oz 2b	A (P) p+p	A (W) pee	S (2.5 hrs)
1:00 - 1:30 pm	S (2 hrs)	S (2 hrs)	A (O)	A (O)	S (2 hrs)	S (2 hrs)	
1:30 - 2:00 pm			S (1.5 hrs)	S (1.5 hrs)			
2:00 - 2:30 pm							
2:30 - 3:00 pm							
3:00 - 3:30 pm	L/S R/S pee/S	p+p		R/S p+p	L/S R/S pee	L/S R/S pee	L/S p+p
3:30 - 4:00 pm	A (P)	A (P)	L/S R/S	L/S	A (O)	A (P)	A (P)
4:00 - 4:30 pm	W	A (O)	A (P)	A (P)	W	W	W
4:30 - 5:00 pm	NAP	NAP	NAP	NAP	NAP	NAP	NAP
5:00 - 5:30 pm			↓	↓			
5:30 - 6:00 pm	3oz 4b	A (P)	2oz (E)	A (E)	3oz 3b	A (F)	2oz 2b
6:00 - 6:30 pm	A (B) p+p	4oz 4b	A (B) pee	3oz 3b	A (B) 3b	3oz 2b	A (B)
6:30 - 7:00 pm	3oz pee	(B)(s) pee	(S)	(B)(s)	3oz p+p	(B)(s) pee	A (B) pee
7:00 - 7:30 pm	S (10 hrs)	4oz	S	6oz	S (11 hrs)	4oz	3oz pee
7:30 - 8:00 pm		S (11.5 hrs)	3oz pee	S (11 hrs)		S (11.5 hrs)	S (12 hrs)
8:00 - 9:00 pm			S (11 hrs)				
9:00 - 10:00 pm							
10:00 - 11:00 pm							
11:00 - 12:00 am							
12:00 - 1:00 am							
1:00 - 2:00 am							
2:00 - 3:00 am							
3:00 - 4:00 am							
4:00 - 5:00 am							
5:00 - 6:00 am							
Total liquids drank	R 3oz L 30	R 3oz L 30	R 3oz L 30	R 3oz L 30	R 3oz L 30	R 3oz L 30	R 3oz L 30
Total solids eaten	7 bites RC	7 bites RC	5 bites RC	10 bites RC	11 bites RC	7 bites RC	10 bites RC
Total poops	2	2	2	2	2	2	2
Total pees	6	6	6	4	5	6	5
Total sleep (night)	10 hrs	10.5 hrs	11 hrs	11 hrs	11 hrs	11.5 hrs	12 hrs
Mom sleep (night)	8 hrs	8 hrs	8 hrs	9 hrs	8 hrs	9 hrs	9 hrs

Comments:
Drop 9 p.m. feeding but baby sometimes wakes at 5 or 5:30 a.m. for breakfast.
Introduced solids - Rice Cereal (RC) - baby is only 26 weeks so only a few bites of solids (b).

Highlight breakfast time, then highlight every three hours after for the rest of the day. Your night feedings will change over time.
Include certain detailed information in your chart every hour or half hour, as applicable.
- Number of minutes per breast and/or ounces of formula. Also include type of solid or liquid and amount of each (bites/oz).
- If vitamins or medicine is given (eg. "D" - if vitamin d is given to baby or "M" medicine, specifying type in the Notes section).
- When baby poops ("poo"), pees ("pee") or both ("p+p").
- If baby pukes more than just a small spit up, including projectile vomit, include "V".
- During baby's awake time, insert "A". If applicable, add "(F)" if she is fussing, "(C)" if crying, or "(S)" if asleep at that time.
  Also insert specific activity, such as "(B)" for bath time, "(P)" for play time, "S" for story time, "(O)" for outing, or "(W)" for a walk.
- When you put baby down to sleep, insert "S". Add "(F)" if she is fussing, "(C)" if crying, or "(A)" if awake during that time.
Keep track of the total amount of solids and liquids, poops and pees, and the amount of sleep you and your baby are getting at night.
In the comments section, make a note of observations about your baby (including if crying a lot) and things like date of new foods introduced, etc.

Note: Baby is beginning to drop late afternoon nap.

Chart for Calmmother feeding and sleep method | calmmother.com | Copyright © Calmmother Limited. All rights reserved.

Note: At a year, switch to sippy cup instead of bottle. Also start to phase out bedtime bottle (switch to goat milk) - baby may need snack (eg yogurt) if no bedtime bottle.

FAQs about the baby feeding and sleep program

When should I start using your feeding and sleep program?

The earlier you start the program after your baby is born the better, especially since it is so gentle (one of our goals is to avoid tears!). If you start immediately after birth your schedule will be the only one your baby will ever know and you should face fewer tears than if you start later. We believe it can cause unnecessary stress and confusion for parents and their baby if a newborn is allowed to feed on demand only to have this schedule change months later!

We don't think it's ever too late to begin the Calmmother feeding and sleep program with your baby. Read Dr. Pam's post about when to start a feeding and sleep program with your baby on our website at www.calmmother.com.

How do I stick with the program when my baby has a cold or is teething?

When your baby isn't feeling well before bed or if they wake up due to a wet or dirty diaper etc., you may find that you need to comfort them before bedtime and/or during the night, especially if they need an extra feeding. In these circumstances you may even find that your baby needs to fall asleep on you. We do not discourage this. However, as noted in our program, this practice may develop into a habit that could result in a deviation from your schedule if you continue to do it consistently.

If you establish your baby's schedule and are generally consistent with feedings and sleep time on day-to-day basis, you will probably find that your baby will go right back to their usual schedule within a day or so after they start to feel better.

Also refer to the homeopathic remedies above.

How should I go about using this program if I start after my baby is a newborn?

Start our program at the phase that most accurately reflects how much your baby is currently sleeping at night. For example, if your baby is waking up every three hours or so, start the program at the first phase. However, if your baby is older, you may be able to fast track through the program in less than 12 weeks by dropping the feedings at night more quickly than if you were starting when your baby was a newborn. Trust your instincts and remember, you can always go back to square one!

We do not recommend starting this program while you are on vacation, or if you have friends or family visiting you. This is because it may be difficult to maintain a consistent schedule, and your baby may be excited, making it more difficult put them down for naps or bedtime.

We think that baby's thrive when they are on a predictable schedule and putting them on a schedule should make them less irritable, generally. But please do not start our program unless your baby is feeling well and is in good health. For example, we would not recommend starting during a time when your baby is particularly irritable due to teething, if they have a cold or flu, or if you are concerned in any way about your baby's health. Consult with your baby's healthcare provider before you start them on any feeding and sleep program.

Unfortunately, the older your baby is when you start sleep training the louder they will be able to cry, not to mention longer! You should be prepared to let your baby cry for longer than the periods referred to in our program (longer than 10 to 15 minutes), unless your healthcare provider suggests otherwise. The older your baby is when you are trying to sleep train them, the harder it can be on you and your baby and the greater the possibility is that you will be faced with tears when you are trying to teach them to fall asleep on their own and/or sleep through the night. This is simply because you may be breaking well-established habits, particularly if they have grown accustomed to waking up in the middle of the night for a snack or snuggle time. This process may very well be harder on you than your baby!

Why should feeding windows be a maximum of 1.5 hours, not longer?

We recommend that you not feed your baby for longer than 1.5 hours from the time you start to avoid overlapping feeding windows. When your baby is a newborn there may be times that you feed them for up to two hours to ensure that they have had a full feeding before you put them down for a nap. However, we do not recommend getting into this habit. A minimum of a 1.5 hour nap in between feedings is ideal when you baby is a newborn to help establish clear feeding windows and to help them begin to distinguish between awake and sleep time.

Why don't you recommend a strict schedule of feeding followed by play time then sleep time during the day?

We think that distinguishing between awake and asleep time is sufficient to help Mothers establish a flexible schedule for their babies. Requiring babies to eat, play and then sleep in that order is unnecessarily complicated, too rigid and not realistic, especially when your baby begins to sleep less during the day (i.e., when they no longer nap, your baby will alternate between play time and feeding time, and perhaps quiet time as well). Newborns typically don't play or really have much awake time at all; if your newborn hasn't fallen asleep on you during their feeding, you may find that they will snuggle on you and fall asleep shortly after they have finished their feeding.

We do however recommend establishing clear feeding windows, half an hour to an hour and a half in length, depending on your baby. Babies tend to be most alert when they wake up after sleep time - this is particularly observable with newborns since they sleep so much. Because of this, you may want to try to feed your newborn as soon as is practicable after they wake up from their nap, based on their chart.

How often should I breastfeed or express milk (using a breast pump) for when my baby starts to sleep eight or more hours at night? I want to make sure that I don't lose my milk supply but don't want to over pump!

The short answer is that this will depend on your milk supply in addition to whether you are either exclusively breastfeeding or expressing, or if you are doing a combination of both. You will probably find that it will be an exercise of trial and error to figure out how much your body will produce and what you are comfortable with in terms of frequency and duration. You may also notice that your supply will increase and decrease depending on your energy level, the amount of rest you are getting and whether or not your nutritional intake is adequate.

Some suggest that the more frequently you breastfeed or express breastmilk the more you will produce, insisting that Mothers should feed or pump at least once every three hours. However, you may find that you can produce a certain amount of milk in a 24 hour period regardless of how often or how long you breastfeed or pump for. Suggestions regarding ways to help increase or reduce your milk supply are outlined in our program.

The specific recommendations below are based in part on the experiences of women who have used our program. A general note is that you may want to be consistent in terms of when you are expressing (i.e., time of day or night), how often you are pumping for and for how long to avoid issues such as engorgement (which really hurts)!

Exclusively breastfeeding

Try to breastfeed your baby at their designated feeding times, based on their chart. When your baby is able to sleep 10 or more hours at night, you may find that you would rather feed them again before you go to bed so that you don't risk losing your milk supply. However, this means that they will only sleep around eight hours from then until you wake them for breakfast. If you prefer to let your baby sleep for 10 or more hours straight at this stage but are concerned about losing your milk supply, consider expressing breastmilk using a breast pump before you go to bed. You don't have to feed your baby the milk you express right away - you could store it in your freezer to use at a later date.

Exclusively expressing breastmilk using a breast pump

We think this is most easily explained when we break it down into phases or stages, based on how long your baby is able to sleep at night:

- *Weeks one to two*, when your baby is feeding approximately every three hours – pump every three hours for 15 to 30 minutes on each breast. Your baby may only drink a few ounces at each feeding during this period but your body will likely produce much more if you tell it to. This can help build your milk supply, and you can always freeze the extra milk to use at a later date.

- *Weeks three to 12*, when your baby begins to sleep for longer periods at night – taper down so that you are consistently pumping once every 4 or 6 hours for 15 to 30 minutes on each breast.

- *Week 12 onward*, when your baby sleeps 10 or more hours at night – consistently pump four times every 24 hours for 15 to 30 minutes on each breast (consider pumping approximately every six hours during the day, including before you go to bed and then eight hours later the following morning).

Combination of breastfeeding and expressing breastmilk using a breast pump

After you have finished breastfeeding your baby, immediately pump for up to 10 minutes on each breast. If you have not just breastfed (i.e., if you are pumping after your baby has already gone to bed for the night), try pumping for 15 to 30 minutes on each breast.

Note that babies are able to get milk from your breasts more effectively than a pump. If you are breastfeeding before you pump, you may not be able to not pump as many ounces as you might like. Also, you may want to pump for longer periods of time as your baby gets older to help ensure that you are consistently producing the same amount of milk each time you breastfeed and/or pump.

My baby was perfectly on schedule then we got off track! How can we get back on schedule again?

Many parents who have used the Calmmother feeding and sleep program schedule have said they got off track at least once before transitioning back on to the schedule again. If you get off schedule, don't get discouraged. Absent health concerns, there is no reason you won't be able to get back on track as long as you don't wait too long to try again!

There are a number of reasons why your baby could get off schedule including growth spurts, teething, health concerns and new habits. Figuring out why your baby is waking up at night is important for determining how to get back on track, especially if you'd like to avoid tears.

Here are our top tips for getting back on schedule:

Figure out why your baby is waking up at night

This is probably the most important factor in determining how to get back on schedule especially if you'd like to avoid tears. There are a number of reasons why your baby could get off schedule including growth spurts, teething, health concerns and new habits. Examples of habits are if they skip naps during the day or stay up too late (and become overtired), if they become accustomed to being held more or rocked to sleep when family or friends are visiting – these types of habits can develop fast, in as little as a day or two, and can be difficult to break especially if they become well-established. Parents should be comfortable with the habits they are creating in their home.

Ensure your baby is having full feedings during the day

It is completely normal for a baby to have a full feeding in 20 minutes at each feeding by the time they are three months or older. But until then we recommend 1.5 hour feedings (including the top up) followed by nap or bedtime unless you are sure that their tummy is full in less time.

Keep consistent with the schedule but always feed your baby when they're hungry?

There may be times when a feeding in the middle of the night is necessary because your baby actually is hungry. This could be because they are going through a growth spurt or simply didn't have enough to drink (or eat, if at the solids stage) during the day! Consult your healthcare provider if you think your baby is waking up because they are ready to start eating solids.

Sometimes you can get away with giving a smaller feeding than usual to your baby if they wake up hungry in the middle of the night, especially if it's within a 3-4 hours of breakfast because a full feeding for breakfast is important. Starting when your baby is about six months old you should be able to adjust their feeding and sleep times by about an hour each way without worrying about meltdowns (i.e., so if they need a night feeding you can push breakfast back by an hour more easily compared to when they are a newborn and are establishing their schedule).

Don't forget top up before bedtime

This feeding should be distinguished from your baby's dinner feeding.

We suggest continuing to give your child a top up before bed until you know for sure that they do not need it, or until your baby is a toddler and has transitioned to a bedtime snack (i.e., sometime around the one year mark when your healthcare provider suggests transitioning from breastmilk/formula to milk).

Although we wholeheartedly promote breastfeeding, some parents we've talked to have observed that formula seems to be a bit more substantial than breastmilk, especially at night. That said, some of the Mothers who have successfully used the Calmmother feeding and sleep program have exclusively fed their babies breastmilk for the first six months. If you are bottle feeding at bedtime around the 4-6 month mark and your baby begins to wake up regularly at night, ask your healthcare provider about adding a spoonful or two of cereal to the breastmilk/formula to make the feeding more substantial. If you do this, don't forget to change the nipple on the bottle to account for the thicker consistency.

When your baby is around a year old, you may prefer to trade the bedtime bottle for a sippy cup to distinguish it as a bedtime snack rather than an actual meal. Depending on your preferences, you may decide to transition to something like yogurt or cereal before bed at this point – jumping ahead to the 18 month or two year mark, fewer liquids before bed can be very helpful for purposes of potty training.

Illnesses, teething and travel can throw a baby off their sleep schedule.

See our site for tips for sticking with the program when your baby is sick, teething and if you are planning to travel with your baby.

Short term crying can mean long-term benefits

At some point you are likely going to have to listen to a bit of crying, especially if your baby is simply waking up out of habit for an extra hug each night. If they do not self soothe within the period you're comfortable with (one to 30 minutes or longer depending on age) pick up your crying baby for a quick hug before putting them down again, firmly letting them know it's sleep time. Repeat this until your baby falls asleep on their own.

When teaching your baby to fall asleep on their own, they will be more likely to cry if they've already gotten used to falling asleep on you (i.e., if they are sound asleep when you lay them in their crib). If you are faced with tears because of this, it may be easier to start the transition after a feeding when you know they're more tired. For example, a feeding in the middle of the night or at bedtime.

Be patient and don't be too hard on yourself or your baby

You and your baby are doing the best you can, enjoy every minute of it!

How does the program work when you are traveling? I don't want to be stuck in my hotel room with a sleeping baby the whole time!

A benefit of our program is that it allows for flexibility, and teaches your baby to be adaptable in terms of where and when they sleep. If your baby was on an established schedule before your trip, they shouldn't have any problem going back to their usual schedule within a day or so after you arrive home, particularly if it is a short trip.

If you are switching time zones, we recommend transitioning your baby to the new time zone as soon as you arrive and switching back to the normal time zone as soon as you get back - you would be surprised how quickly babies can adapt. Note that you may want to move your baby's schedule forward or back 15 minutes a day for the few days or week prior to departure to help them transition upon arrival at your new destination, though we don't think this is necessary. If the time zone difference is more than four hours, you may need to add extra feedings while you transitioning them to the new time zone (plus, airplane rides can be very dehydrating!).

If you are only away for a few days, you may not need to worry about your baby getting off of their established schedule for those days (i.e., missing a few naps or eating earlier or later than usual). They may be a bit overtired when you get home, but longer naps (or a few extra naps) for a few days following your arrival should do the trick when getting them back on track.

If you plan on being away for longer than a few days and know that your baby will miss naps or be up later at night on a regular basis, consider sticking with the established schedule every second or third day to help avoid mixing up the schedule you have worked so hard to establish.

Acknowledgments

A special thank you to all of the amazing Mothers who have contributed to this book!

With deepest gratitude, thank you to our loved ones who have been and continue to share in their journey with us. You know who you are and we are eternally grateful for your love and support.

Made in the USA
Monee, IL
18 June 2020